The New Rules for Retirement Income

Guaranteed Strategies for Today's Retirees

By Jeff Weidner
Boom Retirement Solutions

Published by Boom Retirement Solutions
Wake Forest, NC

Limited Liability and Disclaimer of Warranty:
Every effort has been made by the author and publisher to ensure the accuracy and completeness of this book. However, the publisher and author make no representations or warranties of any kind, express or implied, about the accuracy or completeness of the contents. They specifically disclaim all implied warranties of merchantability or fitness for a particular purpose.

The strategies and advice in this book may not be suitable for every situation. Neither the author nor the publisher shall be held liable for any loss of profit or other damages, including but not limited to special, incidental, consequential, or other damages arising out of the use or misuse of the information provided. Readers should consult with a qualified professional for personalized guidance.

Description:
First Edition
Published in Wake Forest, NC by Boom Retirement Solutions, 2025

Summary:
This guide provides the new rules for creating passive retirement income that every retiree should know to reduce tax liabilities, minimize Required Minimum Distributions (RMDs), and achieve lasting financial success in retirement.

Author: Jeff Weidner

Dedication

To all those approaching retirement, may you find the confidence and clarity to make the most of your retirement assets, reduce your taxes and create the retirement you deserve.

And to my family, whose support made this book possible.

Acknowledgments
Writing a book about Retirement Income that is both comprehensive and accessible requires the support and expertise of many individuals. I would like to express my deepest gratitude to:

My clients, whose questions and concerns helped shape the content of this book. Your trust in me to guide you through retirement planning decisions has been both a privilege and an inspiration.

The team at Boom Retirement Solutions, whose dedication to serving our clients with excellence provides the foundation for everything we do. Your commitment to helping people create secure retirement income strategies makes our work meaningful and impactful.

My mentors in the financial services industry taught me the importance of putting clients first and always continuing to learn. Your guidance has been invaluable in developing the expertise shared in these pages.

The editorial team, whose careful attention to detail helped ensure this complex subject matter is presented clearly and accurately. Your contributions have made this book more accessible and useful for readers.

My family, whose patience and support during the writing process made this book possible. Your encouragement kept me going through long hours of research and writing. Finally, to you, the reader, for taking this important step toward understanding and maximizing your income in retirement. Your commitment to creating a secure retirement future is admirable.

acknowledgments

Writing a book about Retirement Income that is both comprehensive and accessible requires the support and expertise of many individuals. I would like to express my deepest gratitude to:

My clients, whose questions and concerns helped shape the content of this book. Your trust in me to guide you through retirement planning decisions has been both a privilege and an inspiration.

[illegible]

[illegible]

[illegible]

[illegible]

How to Use This Book

Retirement income planning isn't what it used to be. With changing tax laws, evolving Social Security rules, and longer life expectancies, you need a guide that cuts through the confusion and empowers you to make informed decisions. *The New Rules for Retirement Income* is your roadmap to creating a secure, sustainable, and predictable financial future.

This book is designed to be both comprehensive and practical, offering clear explanations, actionable strategies, and real-world examples. Here's how to get the most out of it:

1. **Start Where You Are**

Each chapter builds on key principles, but you don't need to read the book cover to cover to benefit. Feel free to skip ahead to topics that are most relevant to your current financial concerns, such as Social Security, tax strategies, or guaranteed income options.

2. **Engage with the Tools and Strategies**

Throughout the book, you'll find checklists, questions to discuss with your advisor, and easy-to-follow steps for implementing the strategies you learn. Use these tools to evaluate your current plan and identify areas for improvement.

3. **Apply the Insights to Your Unique Situation**

No two retirement plans are alike. As you read, think about how the concepts apply to your goals, family situation, and financial circumstances. Highlight key points, jot down notes, and revisit sections as your needs evolve.

4. **Take Action**

Knowledge without action won't secure your retirement. At the end of each chapter, you'll find specific actions you can take right now to start building a stronger retirement income plan. Use these as a checklist to guide your progress.

5. **Consult with Professionals When Needed**

While this book is packed with expert insights, it's not a substitute for personalized advice. Use what you learn here as a foundation for meaningful discussions with financial advisors, tax professionals, or estate planners.

By using this book as your go-to resource, you'll gain clarity, confidence, and control over your retirement income. Whether you're five years from retirement or already navigating this new chapter of life, *The New Rules for Retirement Income* will help you create the financial freedom and security you deserve.

Table of Contents

Introduction: The New Rules for Retirement Income

Sarah Jensen stared at her retirement account statement in disbelief. After decades of following the traditional advice of maxing out her 401(k) and planning for the standard 4% withdrawal, she realized her plan wasn't built for today's economic realities. Market volatility, rising healthcare costs, and longer life expectancies had eroded the foundations of her financial security. Sarah isn't alone. Thousands of retirees and soon-to-be retirees are finding that the old rules no longer work. That's where this book comes in.

Welcome to *The New Rules for Retirement Income.* This book is your guide to navigating the challenges of modern retirement and building a plan that provides guaranteed income and peace of mind. Whether you're just beginning to plan for retirement, have recently retired, or are seeking ways to optimize your current strategy, you'll find the tools and insights you need to secure your financial future.

Introducing the Six Key Personas

To make these strategies more relatable, this book introduces six personas, each representing a unique retirement journey. As you read, you may find yourself in one or more of these characters, each facing distinct challenges and goals.

1. The Near-Retiree Planner

Meet Tom, a 58-year-old engineer who plans to retire in seven years. He's diligently saved in his 401(k) but worries it won't be enough. Tom is navigating questions about Social Security, tax efficiency, and how to protect his savings from market downturns. He represents those who want to build a robust retirement foundation before taking the leap.

2. The Recent Retiree Adjuster

Barbara, a 63-year-old former teacher, retired two years ago. While she's enjoying her freedom, the rollercoaster of market volatility has shaken her confidence. She's seeking strategies to stabilize her income and ensure her savings last as long as she does.

3. The Established Retiree Optimizer

David and Lisa, both in their early 70s, have been retired for nearly a decade. Their investments have performed well, but they're increasingly concerned about taxes on their RMDs and rising healthcare costs. They're looking to fine-tune their plan to preserve their lifestyle and protect their legacy.

4. The Risk-Averse Safety Seeker

Meet Susan, a 66-year-old widow who's extremely cautious with her money. Her primary goal is to avoid losses while ensuring her basic expenses are covered. Susan represents those who value security above all and are exploring options like annuities for guaranteed income.

5. The Long-Term Visionary

Michael, a 54-year-old business owner, is forward-thinking about retirement. He's actively exploring Roth conversions, tax-smart investing, and long-term care planning. Michael knows that early preparation can create a retirement that's not only secure but also abundant.

6. The Long-Lived Optimist

Margaret is a 92-year-old widow who has been retired for nearly 30 years. When she first retired at 65, she planned for a 20-year retirement, believing it would be more than sufficient. But Margaret's longevity has far exceeded her expectations, and she now faces challenges she hadn't anticipated, such as rising healthcare costs, outliving her original savings plan, and maintaining her independence.

Why the Old Rules No Longer Work

The retirement landscape has fundamentally shifted. Here's why:

- **Longevity:** Retirements often last 25-30 years or more, placing unprecedented demands on savings.
- **Market Volatility:** The ups and downs of the stock market can wreak havoc on portfolios during withdrawal years.
- **Taxes:** RMDs, Social Security taxation, and potential future tax increases pose significant challenges.
- **Healthcare Costs:** With medical expenses rising faster than inflation, retirees need strategies to manage these costs.

PART 1: THE NEW RETIREMENT LANDSCAPE

Chapter 1: Today's Retirement Challenges

Retirement today is not what it used to be. The strategies that worked for previous generations—like relying on pensions, Social Security, and simple withdrawal plans—are no longer enough. Modern retirees face a new set of challenges: longer lifespans, market volatility, rising healthcare costs, and the triple threat of taxes, inflation, and unexpected expenses.

Let's explore these challenges through the experiences of six personas, each navigating their unique retirement journey. You'll likely see yourself reflected in one or more of them.

Living Longer: The Longevity Challenge

Here's an exciting fact: we're living longer than ever before. Thanks to better medicine and healthier lifestyles, many of us will live well into our 80s or 90s. That's wonderful news! But it also creates a unique challenge – making sure your money lasts as long as you do.

Think about these numbers:

- In 1960, the average retirement lasted just 8 years
- Today, many retirements last 25-30 years

- Some people will spend more time retired than they did working

It's like running a marathon, but you don't know where the finish line is. You need to pace yourself and carry enough water to finish the race.

Tom, a Near-Retiree Planner, is 58 years old and aiming to retire by 65. He's diligently saved in his 401(k), but as he thinks about the possibility of living well into his 90s, he worries: *Will my savings last for 30 years or more?* Tom's financial advisor recently told him, *Retirement is like running a marathon, but you don't know where the finish line is.* That uncertainty drives his desire to create a plan with built-in flexibility and guaranteed income.

Barbara, a Recent Retiree Adjuster, retired two years ago at 63. She's already feeling the impact of longevity in unexpected ways. Rising healthcare costs and her desire to travel frequently are straining her initial budget. She reflects, *I thought I'd only need 70% of my working income, but I'm spending as much, if not more, than I did before retiring.*

Longevity isn't just about how long you'll live; it's about how well you can sustain your lifestyle over time. Planning for this means ensuring your money lasts as long as you do, with safeguards in place for the unexpected.

The Three Big Questions About Longevity:

1. How long might you live?
2. How much money will you need?
3. What happens if you live even longer than expected?

Let's tackle each question with real examples.

How Long Might You Live? Look at your family history. Do your parents or grandparents live into their 90s? There are millions of retirees that never expected to reach 85. Now they're worried about running out of money because they planned for a 20-year retirement, not 30 years.

How Much Money Will You Need? The old rule said you needed 70% of your working income in retirement. That rule is outdated. Today's retirees often need 100% or more. Why? Because they're:

- More active
- Traveling more
- Facing higher healthcare costs
- Supporting adult children or grandchildren

What If You Live Even Longer? This is where guaranteed income becomes crucial. You need money you can't outlive, no matter what.

Market Volatility and Your Retirement

Remember 2008? How about early 2020? These market drops taught us an important lesson: market volatility can wreck retirement plans.

Linda Martinez learned this the hard way. She had $800,000 saved when she retired in 2007. By 2009, her savings had dropped to $460,000. This was an above average loss of 42.5% because she was still 100% invested in various stocks. She failed to take any action to reduce her risk when she entered retirement. She had to go back to work part-time. It's like hiking up a mountain when a sudden storm hits – you need shelter from the storm. She is wondering what steps she should take to protect her retirement nest egg before the next market collapse. She knows that last time she failed to plan properly, and she will not make that mistake again.

Susan, a Risk-Averse Safety Seeker, remembers the 2008 financial crisis vividly. Watching her retirement savings drop by 30% back then left her determined to protect herself from future market swings. Now 66, she's avoided significant stock market exposure, but she worries: *Am I missing out on growth?* She's beginning to explore options like Fixed Indexed Annuities to create a reliable income floor that will protect her from volatility while providing modest growth.

David and Lisa, Established Retiree Optimizers in their early 70s, learned about sequence of returns risk the hard way. Early in their retirement, they experienced a major market downturn that forced them to sell investments at a loss to cover expenses. While their portfolio has recovered since, they've adjusted their strategy. Now, they keep two years' worth of essential expenses in cash reserves and rely on guaranteed income sources for their monthly needs, reducing their dependence on market performance.

Market volatility doesn't just affect your net worth; it can derail your income plan if not managed properly. Strategies like diversifying income sources and creating a cash buffer can protect your retirement from these risks.

Understanding Market Risk in Retirement:

- Market drops hurt more when you're taking withdrawals
- You have less time to recover from losses
- Traditional diversification might not be enough

Let's talk about sequence of returns risk. Don't worry if this sounds complicated – we'll make it simple.

Meet Bob and Sue. They both start with $500,000. They both withdraw $25,000 a year. They both earn the same average return over 20 years. The only difference? Bob faces bad markets early in retirement, while Sue faces them later. Bob runs out of money at age 83. Sue has plenty left. That's sequence of returns risk in action.

DECUMULATION PHASE | $50,000 A YEAR DISTRIBUTIONS
FIRST 3 YEARS POSITIVE RETURNS | LAST 3 YEARS NEGATIVE RETURNS

Bob's PORTFOLIO A

Age	Annual Return	Starting Balance	Withdrawal $50K/Yr	Ending Balance
65		$ 500,000		$ 500,000
66	-25%	$ 375,000	$ 25,000.00	$ 350,000
67	-14%	$ 301,000	$ 25,000.00	$ 276,000
68	-10%	$ 248,400	$ 25,000.00	$ 223,400
69	16%	$ 259,144	$ 25,000.00	$ 234,144
70	21%	$ 283,314	$ 25,000.00	$ 258,314
71	5%	$ 271,230	$ 25,000.00	$ 246,230
72	-16%	$ 206,833	$ 25,000.00	$ 181,833
73	8%	$ 196,380	$ 25,000.00	$ 171,380
74	14%	$ 195,373	$ 25,000.00	$ 170,373
75	24%	$ 211,263	$ 25,000.00	$ 186,263
76	14%	$ 212,339	$ 25,000.00	$ 187,339
77	5%	$ 196,706	$ 25,000.00	$ 171,706
78	-15%	$ 145,950	$ 25,000.00	$ 120,950
79	-26%	$ 89,503	$ 25,000.00	$ 64,503
80	22%	$ 78,694	$ 25,000.00	$ 53,694
81	23%	$ 66,044	$ 25,000.00	$ 41,044
82	16%	$ 47,610	$ 25,000.00	$ 22,610
83	9%	$ 24,645	$ 25,000.00	$ (355)
84	23%	$ (436)		$ (436)
85	19%	$ (519)		$ (519)
86	20%	$ (623)		$ (623)
87	-5%	$ (592)		$ (592)
88	22%	$ (722)		$ (722)
89	28%	$ (924)		$ (924)
90	5%	$ (970)		$ (970)

7.32% Avg % Rate

$ 25,000.00 Avg Withdrawal

DECUMULATION PHASE | $50,000 A YEAR DISTRIBUTIONS
FIRST 3 YEARS POSITIVE RETURNS | LAST 3 YEARS NEGATIVE RETURNS

Sue's PORTFOLIO B

Age	Annual Return	Starting Balance	Withdrawal $50K/Yr	Ending Balance
65		$ 500,000		$ 500,000
66	5%	$ 525,000	$ 25,000.00	$ 500,000
67	28%	$ 640,000	$ 25,000.00	$ 615,000
68	22%	$ 750,300	$ 25,000.00	$ 725,300
69	-5%	$ 689,035	$ 25,000.00	$ 664,035
70	20%	$ 796,842	$ 25,000.00	$ 771,842
71	19%	$ 918,492	$ 25,000.00	$ 893,492
72	23%	$ 1,098,995	$ 25,000.00	$ 1,073,995
73	9%	$ 1,170,655	$ 25,000.00	$ 1,145,655
74	16%	$ 1,328,959	$ 25,000.00	$ 1,303,959
75	23%	$ 1,603,870	$ 25,000.00	$ 1,578,870
76	22%	$ 1,926,222	$ 25,000.00	$ 1,901,222
77	-26%	$ 1,406,904	$ 25,000.00	$ 1,381,904
78	-15%	$ 1,174,618	$ 25,000.00	$ 1,149,618
79	5%	$ 1,207,099	$ 25,000.00	$ 1,182,099
80	14%	$ 1,347,593	$ 25,000.00	$ 1,322,593
81	24%	$ 1,640,016	$ 25,000.00	$ 1,615,016
82	14%	$ 1,841,118	$ 25,000.00	$ 1,816,118
83	8%	$ 1,961,407	$ 25,000.00	$ 1,936,407
84	-16%	$ 1,626,582	$ 25,000.00	$ 1,601,582
85	5%	$ 1,681,661	$ 25,000.00	$ 1,656,661
86	21%	$ 2,004,560	$ 25,000.00	$ 1,979,560
87	16%	$ 2,296,289	$ 25,000.00	$ 2,271,289
88	-10%	$ 2,044,161	$ 25,000.00	$ 2,019,161
89	-14%	$ 1,736,478	$ 25,000.00	$ 1,711,478
90	-25%	$ 1,283,609	$ 25,000.00	$ 1,258,609

7.32% Avg % Rate

$ 25,000.00 Avg Withdrawal

Now take the same scenario but instead of taking a fixed rate of $25,000 a year this time we will have them take 4%.

DECUMULATION PHASE | 4% A YEAR DISTRIBUTIONS
FIRST 3 YEARS POSITIVE RETURNS | LAST 3 YEARS NEGATIVE RETURNS

Bob's PORTFOLIO A

Age	Annual Return	Starting Balance	Withdrawal %	Ending Balance
65		$ 500,000	4%	$ 500,000
66	-25%	$ 375,000	$ 20,000.00	$ 355,000
67	-14%	305300	$ 14,200.00	$ 291,100
68	-10%	$ 261,990	$ 11,644.00	$ 250,346
69	16%	$ 290,401	$ 10,013.84	$ 280,388
70	21%	$ 339,269	$ 11,215.50	$ 328,053
71	5%	$ 344,456	$ 13,122.14	$ 331,334
72	-16%	$ 278,321	$ 13,253.36	$ 265,067
73	8%	$ 286,273	$ 10,602.69	$ 275,670
74	14%	$ 314,264	$ 11,026.79	$ 303,237
75	24%	$ 376,014	$ 12,129.47	$ 363,884
76	14%	$ 414,828	$ 14,555.37	$ 400,273
77	5%	$ 420,286	$ 16,010.90	$ 404,275
78	-15%	$ 343,634	$ 16,171.01	$ 327,463
79	-26%	$ 242,323	$ 13,098.52	$ 229,224
80	22%	$ 279,653	$ 9,168.96	$ 270,484
81	23%	$ 332,696	$ 10,819.38	$ 321,876
82	16%	$ 373,377	$ 12,875.06	$ 360,502
83	9%	$ 392,947	$ 14,420.07	$ 378,527
84	23%	$ 465,588	$ 15,141.07	$ 450,447
85	19%	$ 536,032	$ 18,017.87	$ 518,014
86	20%	$ 621,617	$ 20,720.55	$ 600,896
87	-5%	$ 570,851	$ 24,035.84	$ 546,815
88	22%	$ 667,115	$ 21,872.62	$ 645,242
89	28%	$ 825,910	$ 25,809.69	$ 800,100
90	5%	$ 840,105	$ 32,004.01	$ 808,101

7.32% Avg % Rate

$ 15,677.15 Avg Withdrawal

DECUMULATION PHASE | 4% A YEAR DISTRIBUTIONS
FIRST 3 YEARS POSITIVE RETURNS | LAST 3 YEARS NEGATIVE RETURNS

Sue's PORTFOLIO B

Age	Annual Return	Starting Balance	Withdrawal %	Ending Balance
65		$ 500,000	4%	$ 500,000
66	5%	$ 525,000	$ 20,000.00	$ 505,000
67	28%	$ 646,400	$ 20,200.00	$ 626,200
68	22%	$ 763,964	$ 25,048.00	$ 738,916
69	-5%	$ 701,970	$ 29,556.64	$ 672,414
70	20%	$ 806,896	$ 26,896.54	$ 780,000
71	19%	$ 928,200	$ 31,199.99	$ 897,000
72	23%	$ 1,103,310	$ 35,879.99	$ 1,067,430
73	9%	$ 1,163,498	$ 42,697.19	$ 1,120,801
74	16%	$ 1,300,129	$ 44,832.04	$ 1,255,297
75	23%	$ 1,544,016	$ 50,211.89	$ 1,493,804
76	22%	$ 1,822,441	$ 59,752.15	$ 1,762,688
77	-26%	$ 1,304,389	$ 70,507.54	$ 1,233,882
78	-15%	$ 1,048,800	$ 49,355.27	$ 999,444
79	5%	$ 1,049,417	$ 39,977.77	$ 1,009,439
80	14%	$ 1,150,760	$ 40,377.55	$ 1,110,383
81	24%	$ 1,376,874	$ 44,415.31	$ 1,332,459
82	14%	$ 1,519,003	$ 53,298.37	$ 1,465,705
83	8%	$ 1,582,961	$ 58,628.20	$ 1,524,333
84	-16%	$ 1,280,440	$ 60,973.33	$ 1,219,467
85	5%	$ 1,280,440	$ 48,778.67	$ 1,231,661
86	21%	$ 1,490,310	$ 49,266.15	$ 1,441,044
87	16%	$ 1,671,611	$ 57,641.75	$ 1,613,969
88	-10%	$ 1,452,572	$ 64,558.76	$ 1,388,013
89	-14%	$ 1,193,691	$ 55,520.53	$ 1,138,171
90	-25%	$ 853,628	$ 45,526.84	$ 808,101

7.32% Avg % Rate

$ 45,004.03 Avg Withdrawal

Taking 4% of the available balance allows Bob's portfolio to last a lot longer. Their average withdrawal amounts are vastly different, as will their lifestyle as Bob will be making over $30,000 a year less that Sue every year during his retirement.

This has nothing to do with how much they saved for retirement. This has everything to do with 1) not taking risk off the table before they retired and 2) They both rolled the dice and gambled, one lost and happened to retire during a market downturn, thereby locking losses on every withdrawal. While Sue's gamble paid off and she retired when the market was on an upswing.

Admittedly these are extreme examples but most portfolios can't handle a 10% loss, let alone a 30% to 40% loss. Right now, as of January 2025, the stock market is projected to be overvalued, based on The Buffet Indicator, by over 208%. This indicated the market is perfect for a potential decline of about 30 to 40%. Unlike more recent drops this next one is expected to be severe and last for 10 to 15 years.

The Triple Threat: Taxes, Inflation, and Healthcare Costs

Think of these as the three thieves of retirement. Each one can steal your financial security if you're not careful.
1. Taxes in Retirement Many people think they'll pay less in taxes when they retire. Often, that's not true. Here's why:

- Required Minimum Distributions (RMDs) start at age 73 for people born up until 1959. People born after Jan 1960 will have RMD's that start at age 75.
- RMDs can push you into higher tax brackets
- Social Security benefits might be taxed
- Tax rates could go up in the future

Every time you take money from your 401(k) or traditional IRA, Uncle Sam wants his share. And once RMDs kick in, you must withdraw money whether you need it or not.

2. Inflation: The Silent Wealth Stealer Inflation is like a silent thief that gradually steals your purchasing power. At 3% inflation, prices double every 24 years. Let's make this real:

Look how prices have changed:

- A gallon of milk in 1990: $2.32
- Today: Over $4.00
- A new car in 1990: $16,000
- Today: Over $35,000

If you need $5,000 a month today, you might need $10,000 a month in 24 years – just to buy the same things!

4. **Healthcare Costs** This is often the biggest surprise in retirement. A healthy 65-year-old couple today might need $315,000 just for healthcare. And that doesn't include long-term care!

Medicare helps, but it doesn't cover everything. You still need to pay for:

- Premiums
- Deductibles
- Copays
- Dental care
- Vision care
- Prescription drugs
- Long-term care

Michael, a Long-Term Visionary, is 54 and still working, but he's already taking proactive steps to combat these challenges. He's begun converting portions of his traditional IRA to a Roth IRA to reduce his future tax burden. He's also researching long-term care insurance and inflation-protected investments to safeguard his retirement savings from rising costs.

Barbara has recently experienced the triple threat firsthand. Her taxes increased when she began taking Required Minimum Distributions (RMDs) from her 401(k), and she's noticed that her grocery and utility bills are higher than ever. On top of that, a surprise dental surgery forced her to dip into her savings. *I'm starting to realize that retirement isn't as predictable as I thought,* she says.

Taxes, inflation, and healthcare costs can significantly erode your retirement savings if left unaddressed. The key is to anticipate these expenses and incorporate strategies like Roth conversions, inflation-protected annuities, and health savings accounts into your plan.

A Persona Perspective: The Shared Challenges of Retirement

As these personas demonstrate, the challenges of modern retirement are universal, but their impacts are deeply personal. Whether it's Tom's fear of outliving his savings, Susan's anxiety about market downturns, or Michael's proactive approach to tackling taxes, every retiree must address these issues in their own way. The good news? There are proven strategies to navigate these challenges, and this book will guide you through them step by step.

Chapter Summary

Longevity: Retirement often lasts 25-30 years or more, requiring careful planning to ensure your money lasts as long as you do.

Market Volatility: Sequence of returns risk can derail your income plan, but strategies like guaranteed income and cash buffers can provide protection.

Taxes, Inflation, and Healthcare Costs: These "triple threats" can erode your savings, but proactive measures like Roth conversions and inflation-protected investments can help mitigate their impact.

Action Steps

- Identify which persona(s) best reflect your current retirement concerns.
- Review your income sources and consider how longevity, market volatility, and rising costs could affect your plan.
- Explore the tools and resources available in this book to address these challenges and begin crafting a retirement strategy tailored to your needs.

Retirement planning isn't just about saving money; it's about creating a strategy that adapts to life's uncertainties. Remember: Understanding today's challenges is the first step to solving them. In the next chapter, we'll explore how to build a retirement foundation that can weather these challenges.

Chapter 2: Building Your Retirement Foundation

Think of retirement planning like building a house. You need a solid foundation before anything else. In this chapter, we'll lay that foundation together.

The Three Core Income Needs

Think of retirement planning like constructing a house. Before adding walls, a roof, or decorations, you need a solid foundation. That foundation ensures everything built on top remains strong, stable, and secure—no matter what storms may come. In this chapter, we'll explore how to create a financial foundation tailored to the unique challenges of modern retirement through the lens of our six personas.

Everyone has three basic types of expenses in retirement. First, you have essential expenses – things you must pay for like food, housing, and utilities. Then there are lifestyle expenses, like travel or hobbies. Finally, you have unexpected expenses, such as home repairs or medical bills.

Every retiree's financial foundation begins with understanding their essential, lifestyle, and emergency expenses:

- Essential Expenses: Housing, food, utilities, insurance, basic healthcare

- Lifestyle Expenses: Travel, hobbies, dining out, gifts, entertainment
- Emergency Expenses: Home repairs, medical bills, family help, unexpected needs

Understanding these three areas is crucial.

Persona Perspectives:

- **Tom (Near-Retiree Planner)** is starting to identify his core income needs. He's calculating his essential monthly expenses and realizes that his current savings may not generate enough guaranteed income. His goal is to ensure he can cover the basics no matter what happens in the market.
- **Barbara (Recent Retiree Adjuster)** has discovered her lifestyle expenses are higher than expected, particularly with travel and increased healthcare premiums. She's now rebalancing her plan to ensure her essentials remain covered without dipping too heavily into her discretionary funds.

Creating Your Personal Income Floor

An income floor provides the stability every retiree needs. It's money you can count on every month, no matter what happens in the stock market. Think of it as your retirement paycheck. For most people, this income comes from Social Security, pensions, and guaranteed income products like Fixed Indexed Annuities. For Tom and Barbara they realized that their monthly income wasn't enough to cover the base essential expenses.

That's where guaranteed income strategies come in. They worked with their respective Retirement Specialists to develop plans for additional guaranteed income to cover the gap between their existing guaranteed income and projected expenses. They used part of their savings to ensure they could always pay their essential bills. This gave them peace of mind.

Remember this important point: Your essential expenses should be covered by guaranteed income sources. Don't leave your basic needs up to chance or the stock market.

Essential vs. Discretionary Spending in Retirement

Let's talk about Barbara's story. Barbara loved to travel, but she worried about spending too much. Once we helped her separate her essential spending from her discretionary spending, everything became clearer.

Persona Perspectives:

- **Barbara**: After tracking her spending for three months, Barbara discovered she was underestimating her essential expenses. By adjusting her plan to focus on guaranteed income for essentials, she's now more confident in managing her discretionary spending.

Barbara 's essential expenses came to $4,000 per month. Her Social Security provided $2,200. That left a $1,800 gap in her essential expenses. We helped her create a plan to fill that gap with guaranteed income. Now she knows her basic needs are always covered.

For discretionary spending, Barbara uses her investment portfolio. In good market years, she takes extra trips. In down years, she scales back. But she never worries about paying her basic bills.

This approach gives you freedom. When your essential expenses are covered by guaranteed income, you can invest the rest of your money for growth. You can take more investment risk with your discretionary money because you know your basics are covered.

Quick-Start Action Guide

David and Lisa Cooper had a common problem. They felt overwhelmed by retirement planning. "*Where do we start?*" they asked. Let's break it down into simple steps.
First, add up your essential monthly expenses. Be honest about what's truly essential. The Coopers thought cable TV was essential until they realized it was costing them over $200 a month plus individual subscriptions to other streaming services and movie channels and they really don't watch that much TV. They moved it to their discretionary spending list. They saved $180 a month by switching to Over-The-Air broadcasting to receive local news and selected 2 movie channel subscriptions.

Next, list all your guaranteed income sources. This usually means Social Security and pensions. The Coopers had combined Social Security of $3,500 per month. They had no pensions.

Now, find your income gap. Subtract your guaranteed income from your essential expenses. This shows how much additional guaranteed income you need. The Coopers needed an extra $2,000 per month to cover their essentials.

Finally, look at your savings and investments. How much guaranteed income could they generate? The Coopers found they could create more than enough guaranteed income to fill their gap. This gave them confidence.

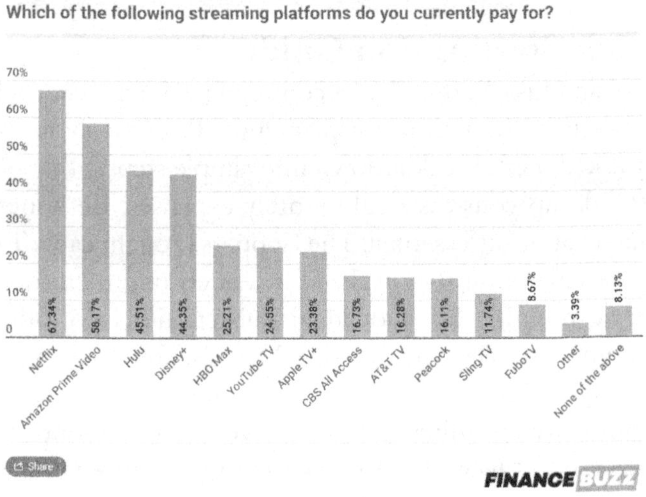

https://financebuzz.com/streaming-survey

Making Your Plan Work

Barbara was worried her plan wouldn't work. "Life changes," she said. "How can I be sure?" Barbara made a good point. Your plan needs to be flexible.

Start with small steps. Barbara began by tracking her spending for three months. This showed her true essential expenses. She was surprised to find she spent less than she thought on some things and more on others.

Review your plan regularly. Barbara checks her budget quarterly. She adjusts when needed. When her property taxes went up, she updated her essential expenses number. Keep some money liquid. Barbara keeps one year of expenses in cash. This gives her flexibility and peace of mind. She doesn't worry about market drops because her essential expenses are covered by guaranteed income.

Actionable Steps to Build Your Foundation

1. **Calculate Your Core Expenses**: Start by listing your essential, lifestyle, and emergency expenses. Be realistic about what you truly need.
2. **Identify Your Guaranteed Income Sources**: Review your Social Security benefits, pensions, and any annuities. Calculate how much of your essential expenses these cover.
3. **Determine Your Income Gap**: Subtract your guaranteed income from your essential expenses. This is the amount you'll need to generate through other strategies.
4. **Create a Reserve Fund**: Set aside liquid savings for emergencies. Aim for six months to one year of essential expenses.
5. **Review and Adjust**: Revisit your plan regularly to account for changing circumstances.

Top 3 Items Readers Will Learn:

1. How to calculate and categorize their essential vs. discretionary expenses
2. Methods to create a guaranteed income floor that covers basic monthly needs
3. Strategies for building and maintaining an appropriate emergency fund in retirement

Building a strong retirement foundation isn't just about having enough savings - it's about creating reliable income streams that will last no matter what the market does. By following the proven strategies outlined in this chapter, you can develop a retirement plan that provides both security for your essential needs and flexibility for your lifestyle goals.

Looking Ahead

Remember, your retirement foundation supports everything else. Take time to get it right.

Think about what you've learned. Separate your expenses into essential and discretionary categories. Find your guaranteed income sources. Calculate your income gap. These steps will build your strong retirement foundation. Your retirement house needs a solid foundation. Take these steps now, and you'll be ready to add the rest of your retirement plan on top of it.

In the next chapter, we'll explore how to protect this foundation from market risks and other threats, ensuring it remains strong and secure for years to come. Let's build on the work you've started and continue crafting the retirement you deserve.

Chapter 3: Protecting Your Retirement Foundation from Market Risks

A strong retirement foundation is only as secure as the protection around it. Imagine building a house on solid ground but leaving the windows open during a storm. The foundation may hold, but the structure could still suffer damage. Market risks, such as volatility and sequence of returns risk, are the storms threatening your retirement. In this chapter, we'll explore how to safeguard your foundation using strategies that address these challenges through the lens of our six personas.

Picture throwing a stone into a pond. The ripples spread outward, affecting more and more of the water's surface. That's how risks work in retirement. One problem can create waves that impact your entire financial future. Let's dive deep into these risks and learn how to protect yourself.

Understanding Market Volatility

The market is unpredictable. It rises and falls for reasons ranging from global events to economic cycles. For retirees, these fluctuations pose a unique challenge: your portfolio may decline in value at the same time you're withdrawing funds. This creates a double hit, making it harder for your savings to recover.

Persona Perspectives:

- **Susan (Risk-Averse Safety Seeker)** remembers vividly how her savings took a sharp hit during the 2008 financial crisis. Since then, she's avoided heavy stock market exposure. But she's beginning to understand that staying completely out of the market may not protect her from inflation, which silently erodes her purchasing power.

Sequence of Returns: The Silent Wealth Killer

Meet Susan. They retired in 2007 with $1 million in savings. Like many retirees, they planned to withdraw $40,000 each year. Then 2008 happened. The market crashed, and their portfolio dropped to $600,000. Even though the market recovered later, their savings never bounced back to $1 million. They had to withdraw money when their accounts were down, leaving less to recover with.

Let's break down exactly what happened to the Susan:

- **2007:** $1,000,000 starting balance
    - Withdrew $40,000 for living expenses
    - Market dropped 38%
    - End of year balance: $600,000
- **2008:** $600,000 starting balance
    - Withdrew $40,000 for living expenses
    - Even with market recovery, they're withdrawing a larger percentage
    - Their portfolio never fully recovered

Persona Perspectives:

- **David and Lisa (Established Retiree Optimizers)** experienced this risk also but were prepared for it. They retired in 2009 with the same $1 million. They also withdrew $40,000 yearly, but they started after the market crash. Today, their portfolio has grown to $1.4 million. Same withdrawal amount, same investment strategy, different timing – dramatically different results. This is sequence of returns risk in real life. It's not just about how much the market goes up or down. It's about when those ups and downs happen and if you are "forced" to lock in losses during a downturn in order to maintain your lifestyle or pay for basic household expenses. Bad returns early in retirement hurt much more than bad returns later.

The Mathematics of Loss

Many people don't realize how hard it is to recover from market losses. Consider these recovery requirements:

- A 20% loss needs a 25% gain to break even.
- A 30% loss needs a 43% gain to break even.
- A 40% loss needs a 67% gain to break even.
- A 50% loss needs a 100% gain to break even.

These may seem like unrealistic losses but based on historical average stock market volatility and returns they are more likely to happen than not. A decline of at least 10% occurred in 10 out of 20 years, or 50% of the time, with an average pullback of 15%. And in two additional years, the decline was just short of 10%.

About 5 years before retirement, it's prudent to start taking risk off the table to avoid sequence of returns risk. When you're withdrawing money during these down periods, the required recovery rates become even higher. This is why Susan struggled to recover despite the market rebound.

Longevity Risk: Why Traditional Plans Fail

"I never thought I'd live this long," Margaret shared recently. Now 92, she's still going strong—well beyond her expectations. Her parents passed away in their 70s, so Margaret planned for a 20-year retirement when she left her career at 65. That was 27 years ago. Today, she's grappling with challenges she never anticipated.

Let's examine the real numbers behind Margaret's situation:

- **Original retirement savings:** $400,000
- **Planned annual withdrawal:** $20,000
- **Expected retirement length:** 20 years
- **Actual retirement length:** 27 years and counting
- **Additional funds needed:** Over $140,000 so far

Margaret's story is a vivid example of why planning for average life expectancy isn't enough. While living longer than expected can be a gift, it also comes with financial stress. Without sufficient planning, outliving your money is a very real risk. Her experience underscores the importance of building flexibility and resilience into your retirement plan to prepare for the unexpected.

The Compounding Effect of Healthcare Costs

Margaret's situation became even more challenging because of rising healthcare costs. When she retired, she spent about $4,000 yearly on healthcare. Now she spends over $12,000 yearly. That's a 200% increase over her retirement years.

Consider these startling healthcare statistics:

- **Average healthcare inflation:** 5.5% annually
- **Regular inflation:** Around 3% annually
- **A 65-year-old couple today might need $315,000 just for healthcare**
- **Long-term care can add another $100,000+ per year**

Strategies to Protect Against Market Risks

1. Diversify Income Sources

Relying solely on market-dependent withdrawals is a recipe for uncertainty. Diversifying your income—with a mix of Social Security, annuities, and pensions—can create stability.

- **Susan** feels more secure knowing her essential expenses are covered by guaranteed income. This allows her to keep a small portion of her savings in the market for potential growth without constant anxiety.

2. Create a Reserve Fund

Having a reserve fund for emergencies or short-term needs can prevent you from selling investments during a downturn. Think of it as your financial storm shelter.

- **Barbara** now maintains a reserve fund with six months of essential expenses. *"Knowing I have this safety net lets me stay patient with the rest of my investments,"* she says.

3. Use Guaranteed Income Products

Products like Fixed Indexed Annuities provide a way to generate reliable income without being exposed to market fluctuations. These can serve as the backbone of your income floor.

- **David and Lisa** have incorporated annuities to cover their monthly essentials, ensuring they're not reliant on selling stocks during volatile periods.

4. Adopt a Bucketing Strategy
Divide your savings into three buckets:

- **Living Bucket for Short-term:** Cash and guaranteed income for the next 1-3 years. This is your guaranteed income for life to cover base monthly living expenses
- **Lifestyle Bucket for Mid-term:** Moderate-risk investments and expenses for the next 4-10 years. This should include discretionary spending items like travel, hobbies etc.
- **Legacy Bucket for Long-term:** Higher-growth investments for expenses beyond 10 years. This could include long term care, setting up trusts, performing Roth conversion or other inheritance vehicles.
- **Tom (Near-Retiree Planner)** from Chapter 2 has embraced this approach, allowing him to confidently invest a portion of his savings in higher-growth assets while knowing his short-term needs are secure.

Actionable Steps to Safeguard Your Retirement

1. **Assess Your Risk Tolerance:** Reflect on how much market risk you can reasonably handle without losing sleep.
2. **Review Your Asset Allocation:** Adjust your portfolio to align with your retirement timeline and goals.
3. **Establish a Reserve Fund:** Set aside 6-12 months of essential expenses in a liquid account.

4. **Incorporate Guaranteed Income:** Explore annuities or similar products to create a stable income floor.
5. **Implement a Bucketing Strategy:** Divide your portfolio into short-, mid-, and long-term buckets to balance risk and reward.

Building Your Risk Defense System

Think of retirement risks like weather threats. You need different protections for different conditions. Here's how the David and Lisa built their risk defense system:

- **Protection Against Market Risk:** They divided their investments into time segments. Money needed in the next five years stayed in safe investments. Longer-term money could go into growth investments.
- **Protection Against Inflation:** They chose investments and income sources that could grow over time. Some of their guaranteed income included inflation adjustments.
- **Protection Against Health Care Costs:** They bought long-term care insurance while they were young enough to qualify for good rates. They also maximized their Health Savings Account contributions.
- **Protection Against Longevity Risk:** They made sure their guaranteed income would last for life, no matter how long they lived. They also kept some money invested for growth to fight inflation.

Your Action Plan

Understanding risks is important. Taking action to protect yourself is essential. Here's what you can do right now:

1. **List your essential expenses.** Be honest about what's truly essential.

2. **Add up your guaranteed income sources.** Know exactly how much you can count on.
3. **Identify your gaps.** How much additional guaranteed income do you need?
4. **Evaluate your savings and investments.** Are you taking more risk than you realized?

Top 3 Items Readers Will Learn:

1. How sequence of returns risk can devastate a retirement portfolio and strategies to mitigate it
2. The mathematics of market losses and why recovery becomes harder in retirement
3. How to implement a bucketing strategy to protect against market volatility while maintaining growth potential

Market risks can derail even the most carefully planned retirement, but with proper protection strategies, you don't have to lie awake at night worrying about your financial security. By implementing the defense systems outlined in this chapter, you can create a retirement plan that's built to weather any market storm while still taking advantage of growth opportunities.

Bringing It All Together

Market risks are an inevitable part of retirement, but they don’t have to derail your plans. By diversifying income sources, creating reserve funds, and incorporating guaranteed income, you can build a plan that weathers any storm. Whether it’s Susan’s need for security, David and Lisa’s experience with sequence of returns risk, or Tom’s proactive planning, each approach offers valuable lessons.

Looking Ahead

In the next chapter, we'll explore specific strategies to maximize your Social Security benefits. This is a crucial part of your guaranteed income foundation.

Remember the pond ripples we talked about at the beginning? Understanding risks helps you see the ripples before the stone is even thrown. Better yet, it helps you protect yourself from their effects.

Your retirement should be a time of confidence and security, not worry and stress. Take time to understand these risks and build your protection strategy. Your future self will thank you.

Chapter 4: Maximizing Social Security

Retirement isn't just about saving; it's about turning those savings into a steady, reliable income stream. The goal is to create a retirement plan that supports your lifestyle while adapting to changes in the economy, taxes, and your personal needs. In this chapter, we'll explore how to optimize your income by balancing growth, safety, and flexibility through the experiences of our six personas.

A stable and adaptable retirement income depends on three core elements: guaranteed income, flexible income, and growth-oriented income. Guaranteed income comes from reliable sources like Social Security, pensions, or annuities that provide consistent payments regardless of market conditions. Flexible income includes investments and accounts that allow for discretionary withdrawals to cover lifestyle and unexpected expenses. Growth-oriented income focuses on long-term investments designed to combat inflation and sustain income over decades.

Think of Social Security like a paycheck you can't outlive. It might be the most important retirement decision you'll make. Yet most people spend more time planning their next vacation than choosing when to take Social Security. Let me show you why this decision matters so much.

The Three Pillars of Optimized Retirement Income

To achieve a stable and adaptable retirement income, it's essential to focus on three core pillars:

1. **Guaranteed Income**: Sources like Social Security, pensions, or annuities that provide consistent payments regardless of market conditions.
2. **Flexible Income**: Investments and accounts that allow for discretionary withdrawals to cover lifestyle and unexpected expenses.
3. **Growth-Oriented Income**: Long-term investments designed to combat inflation and sustain income over decades.

Persona Perspectives:

- **Susan (Risk-Averse Safety Seeker)** relies heavily on guaranteed income sources to cover her essential expenses. Knowing her basics are secure allows her to enjoy retirement without worrying about market volatility.
- **Michael (Long-Term Visionary)** balances all three pillars, ensuring that his investments grow steadily while his Roth IRA provides flexibility for unexpected costs.

Maximizing Social Security Benefits

Social Security is often the cornerstone of guaranteed retirement income, but timing matters. Deciding when to start benefits can significantly impact the total amount you receive over your lifetime.

Persona Perspectives:

- **David and Lisa (Established Retiree Optimizers)** decided to delay claiming Social Security until age 70, maximizing their monthly benefits. This decision provides them with a higher income floor, reducing the pressure on their investments.
- **Tom (Near-Retiree Planner)** is weighing his options. By working a few extra years, he could increase his benefits while continuing to contribute to his savings.

Key Strategies:

- Delay claiming benefits if possible to maximize payouts.
- Coordinate spousal benefits to ensure the highest possible survivor benefit.
- Use tools like the Social Security Administration's calculator to plan effectively.
-

Diversifying Income Streams

Relying on a single income source can be risky. Diversification provides stability and reduces the impact of unforeseen challenges.

Persona Perspectives:

- **Barbara (Recent Retiree Adjuster)** has started diversifying her income by supplementing her Social Security with dividends from her brokerage account and a small annuity.
- **Margaret (Long-Lived Optimist)** learned this lesson the hard way. Outliving her planned income sources, she's now exploring ways to leverage the equity in her home through a reverse mortgage to sustain her lifestyle.

Managing Taxes on Retirement Income

Taxes can significantly erode your retirement income if not managed carefully. Strategies like Roth conversions and tax-efficient withdrawals can help minimize this impact.

Persona Perspectives:

- **Michael** has been converting portions of his traditional IRA to a Roth IRA each year, reducing his future tax burden while keeping his tax rate manageable.
- **Susan** is cautious about taking withdrawals from taxable accounts first to minimize her overall tax liability.

Key Strategies:

- Use Roth accounts for tax-free growth and withdrawals.
- Time withdrawals strategically to stay in lower tax brackets.
- Consider the tax impact of Required Minimum Distributions (RMDs) and plan accordingly.

Incorporating Inflation Protection

Inflation is the silent thief of retirement savings, eroding purchasing power over time. Ensuring your income keeps pace with rising costs is critical for long-term security.

Persona Perspectives:

- **David and Lisa** have allocated a portion of their investments to Treasury Inflation-Protected Securities (TIPS) to guard against inflation.
- **Barbara** is using a Fixed Indexed Annuity with an inflation rider, ensuring her income increases alongside living costs.

Actionable Steps for Optimizing Your Income

1. **Evaluate Your Income Sources**: Determine how much of your income is guaranteed, flexible, and growth-oriented.

2. **Maximize Social Security**: Use tools to calculate the best claiming strategy for your situation.
3. **Diversify and Adjust**: Ensure you're not overly reliant on any single income stream.
4. **Manage Taxes**: Work with a financial advisor or tax professional to minimize the tax burden on your withdrawals.
5. **Account for Inflation**: Incorporate inflation-protected investments or income products into your plan.

Understanding Your Full Retirement Age

Tom, the Near-Retiree Planner, had been confused about his full retirement age. "I thought it was 65, but my neighbor said it's 67. Who's right?" he asked. The answer depends on when you were born. For those born between 1943 and 1954, full retirement age is 66. If you were born in 1960 or later, it's 67. For everyone in between, it's somewhere in the middle.

What truly matters is how long you wait to claim benefits. Every month you delay claiming Social Security after age 62 increases your benefit. David and Lisa, the Established Retiree Optimizers, learned this lesson the hard way. They claimed early at 62 because they could. Now, at age 75, they regret their decision every month as they see the permanent 25% reduction in their Social Security checks.

When Life Throws You Curves

Sometimes life doesn't go as planned. Barbara, the Recent Retiree Adjuster, found herself widowed at 60 and unsure of her options. She thought she needed to wait until 66 to claim any benefits, but that misunderstanding could have cost her thousands. With careful research, Barbara learned she could claim survivor benefits at 60 while allowing her own benefit to grow until age 70. This strategy provided her with crucial income when she needed it most and set her up for larger payments later. Thanks to smart planning, Barbara secured an extra $1,200 in monthly income for life.

Margaret, the Long-Lived Optimist, also faced an unexpected challenge. At 92, she reflects on how she's outlived her initial retirement plan by seven years. Her parents had shorter lifespans, and she didn't expect to live this long. Adjustments, such as tapping into home equity and careful budgeting, have kept her financially afloat, but Margaret's story is a reminder to plan for the unexpected.

The Working Person's Dilemma

Susan, the Risk-Averse Safety Seeker, faced a tough decision when she considered working past age 62. "Can I collect Social Security while working part-time?" she wondered. The answer depends on your earnings. If you claim before your full retirement age and earn above a certain threshold, your benefits may be reduced.

Michael, the Long-Term Visionary, understood this and waited until his full retirement age to claim benefits. By doing so, he avoided any penalties and kept his full Social Security check while continuing to earn a salary. His patience allowed him to maximize both his earnings and retirement benefits, a strategy that has significantly enhanced his financial security.

Marriage, Divorce, and Your Benefits

Social Security rules around marriage and divorce can be surprisingly generous. Margaret learned this late in life. Having been married for over 10 years before divorcing, she discovered she could claim spousal benefits based on her ex-husband's record. This increased her monthly check by $700, a welcome addition to her income. Importantly, this decision didn't affect her ex-husband's benefits at all.

David and Lisa also used marital benefits to their advantage. Lisa claimed her benefits at full retirement age while David delayed his until age 70, ensuring a higher survivor benefit for Lisa in case he passed first. This thoughtful planning added over $200,000 to their lifetime Social Security income and secured Lisa's financial future.

The Tax Trap No One Talks About

Taxes can catch retirees by surprise. Susan's part-time job pushed her Social Security benefits into a higher tax bracket, causing up to 85% of her benefits to become taxable. She learned this the hard way, but David and Lisa took a proactive approach. By coordinating their withdrawals from Roth IRAs and taxable accounts, they minimized their tax burden and kept more of their Social Security income.

Michael has also benefited from planning. By converting portions of his traditional IRA to a Roth IRA, he reduced his taxable income, ensuring he could avoid this common tax trap while maintaining financial flexibility.

Real Numbers, Real Decisions

To make informed decisions, understanding the financial impact of claiming Social Security at different ages is critical. Margaret worked through these numbers with her advisor:

- Claiming at 62 would have provided $1,800 monthly, but by 90, she'd have received $604,800.
- Claiming at 66 increased her benefit to $2,400 monthly, totaling $696,000 by 90.
- Waiting until 70 raised her monthly payment to $3,168, resulting in $793,008 by 90.

The difference between claiming early and waiting until 70 was $188,208. For Margaret, the decision to wait transformed her retirement lifestyle, giving her peace of mind and financial security well into her later years.

Top 3 Items Readers Will Learn:

1. How delaying Social Security benefits increases monthly payments and can provide significant lifetime value
2. Strategies for married couples to maximize their combined benefits, including spousal and survivor benefits
3. Ways to minimize taxes on Social Security benefits through careful income planning and withdrawal strategies

Social Security claiming might be the most important financial decision you make in retirement, potentially worth hundreds of thousands of dollars in lifetime benefits. Understanding the strategies outlined in this chapter can help you avoid costly mistakes and maximize this crucial retirement income source, ensuring greater financial security throughout your retirement years.

Planning for Tomorrow

Michael's proactive approach serves as a model for anyone preparing for Social Security. By starting early, understanding the rules, and aligning Social Security with other retirement income sources, you can maximize your benefits. Whether it's through delaying claims, optimizing spousal strategies, or managing taxes, each step you take brings you closer to financial confidence.

In the next chapter, we'll address how to integrate these strategies with healthcare planning and other essential aspects of a secure retirement.

Chapter 5: The Power of Guaranteed Income

Guaranteed income is the cornerstone of a secure retirement. In a world where pensions are disappearing and market volatility threatens traditional portfolios, having a reliable income source can bring peace of mind and financial stability. In this chapter, we'll explore how modern annuity solutions, income riders, and personal pensions can transform your retirement strategy through the experiences of our six personas.

Understanding Today's Income Challenge

Remember when most people retired with pensions? Those days are largely gone. Today, we're responsible for creating our own retirement paycheck. The challenge isn't just saving money – it's turning those savings into reliable income that lasts a lifetime.

Barbara stared at her 401(k) statement every month. Despite having saved $800,000, she couldn't shake one fear: running out of money. The stock market's ups and downs kept her awake at night. She needed something more reliable than hope.

Let me share what Barbara discovered. She learned that by turning part of her savings into guaranteed income, she could stop worrying about market crashes. Her essential expenses would be covered no matter what. This changed her entire outlook on retirement.

Modern Annuity Solutions

Annuities have evolved significantly over the years. Today's options are more flexible, transparent, and tailored to individual needs than ever before. For Susan, the Risk-Averse Safety Seeker, an annuity was a natural choice. She wanted to ensure her essential expenses were always covered, no matter what happened in the market. Her

Fixed Indexed Annuity provided her with both stability and the potential for modest growth without exposure to market losses.

David and Lisa, the Established Retiree Optimizers, chose a hybrid annuity that offered long-term care benefits. This solution allowed them to address two concerns simultaneously: guaranteed income for life and coverage for potential healthcare costs. "It felt like we were solving two problems with one product," Lisa explained.

Fixed Indexed Annuities Explained

Fixed Indexed Annuities (FIAs) are a popular choice for retirees seeking growth potential and protection. Unlike traditional fixed annuities, FIAs offer interest credits tied to the performance of a market index, such as the S&P 500, while protecting the principal from market downturns. For Margaret, the Long-Lived Optimist, this combination was ideal. At 92, she appreciates the security her annuity provides while still benefiting from occasional market upswings.

Michael, the Long-Term Visionary, researched FIAs extensively before incorporating them into his portfolio. "I liked that I could participate in some market growth without risking my principal," he said. For Michael, the annuity serves as a complement to his other growth-oriented investments, offering balance and security.

Income Riders Worth Considering

Income riders can enhance the value of annuities by providing guaranteed income streams that last a lifetime. Barbara, the Recent Retiree Adjuster, added an income rider to her FIA. This ensured she could count on a steady paycheck throughout her retirement, even if the rest of her savings were depleted. "It's like getting a raise every year," she remarked, referring to the annual increase in her guaranteed payments.

Tom, the Near-Retiree Planner, also found income riders appealing. As someone nearing retirement, he wanted to lock in a guaranteed income that would start immediately upon retiring. "I didn't want to worry about running out of money," he said. The rider gave him the confidence to retire on his own terms.

The Power of Sleep-at-Night Money

David and Lisa learned about guaranteed income the hard way. During the 2020 market crash, their stock market investment-only approach meant sleepless nights and constant worry. They had planned to take 4% a year off of their retirement accounts to pay all of their expenses. When the market took that sudden drop, and they needed to put a new roof on their house they were forced to lock in losses. That $15,000 roof cost them approximately $40,000 in future retirement growth. They didn't have cash reserves, and they didn't have a guaranteed income stream to cover their base monthly expenses. It was a tough lesson to learn.

Think about your monthly bills. You have utilities, food, healthcare premiums, property taxes. These expenses don't care what the stock market does. They need to be paid regardless. That's why guaranteed income is so crucial.

Let me show you what this means in real numbers. David and Lisa had saved $1 million for retirement. Like most people, they thought this meant they could withdraw $40,000 a year safely. But some years, taking out that $40,000 meant selling investments at the worst possible time.

There is a better way. They calculated their essential expenses: $4,000 monthly. Their Social Security would provide $3,000. This left a $1,000 monthly gap. Instead of hoping their investments would generate this income, they created guaranteed income to fill the gap plus a little extra that they used to bolster their cash accounts.

Building Your Personal Pension

For many retirees, the idea of a personal pension is both comforting and practical. With fewer employers offering defined benefit pensions, creating your own through annuities is an effective way to ensure lifetime income. Susan used an annuity to create her personal pension, knowing it would cover her housing, utilities, and food costs. "I know my basics are always covered," she said. Margaret's personal pension allowed her to maintain her independence. "I don't have to rely on my kids for financial help," she shared. Her annuity provides her with enough income to cover her essentials while preserving her other assets for discretionary spending and emergencies.

When Guaranteed Income Makes Sense

Michael: The Long Term Visionary thought guaranteed income products weren't for him. "I can invest my money and get better returns," he said. Then I showed him something that changed his mind.

In retirement, it's not just about returns. It's about reliable income. Michael needed $5,000 monthly for comfortable retirement. Social Security would provide $2,800. To generate the extra $2,200 from investments alone, he'd need to take significant market risk.

Instead, Michael used part of his savings to create guaranteed income. This gave him two advantages. First, he knew his essential expenses were covered for life. Second, he could invest his remaining money more aggressively for growth.

The Legacy Question

"But what about leaving money to our kids?" That's what David and Lisa asked me. It's a common concern with guaranteed income strategies. The answer surprised the two of them.

By using guaranteed income for essential expenses, they could actually invest their remaining money more aggressively for growth. This money could grow for his legacy goals while his guaranteed income covered his needs. They didn't have to choose between security and leaving a legacy – he could do both.

Actionable Steps to Leverage Guaranteed Income

1. **Evaluate Your Needs**: Determine how much of your essential expenses should be covered by guaranteed income.
2. **Research Annuity Options**: Compare fixed, variable, and indexed annuities to find the best fit for your goals.
3. **Consider Income Riders**: Explore riders that provide lifetime income, inflation adjustments, or spousal benefits.
4. **Build Your Personal Pension**: Work with a financial professional to structure an annuity that meets your retirement needs.

Top 3 Items Readers Will Learn:

1. How sequence of returns risk can devastate a retirement portfolio and strategies to mitigate it
2. The mathematics of market losses and why recovery becomes harder in retirement
3. How to implement a bucketing strategy to protect against market volatility while maintaining growth potential.

Market risks can derail even the most carefully planned retirement, but with proper protection strategies, you don't have to lie awake at night worrying about your financial security. By implementing the defense systems outlined in this chapter, you can create a retirement plan that's built to weather any market storm while still taking advantage of growth opportunities.

Top 3 Items Readers Will Learn:

1. How to create a personal pension using modern annuity products
2. Ways to balance guaranteed income with growth potential to combat inflation
3. Strategies for covering essential expenses while maintaining investment flexibility for discretionary spending

In a world where traditional pensions are disappearing and market volatility can threaten retirement security, creating your own guaranteed income stream is more crucial than ever. The strategies in this chapter show you how to build reliable retirement paychecks that last a lifetime, giving you the freedom to enjoy retirement without worrying about market crashes or outliving your money.

Bringing It All Together

The power of guaranteed income lies in its ability to provide stability in an unpredictable world. Whether it's Susan securing her essentials, Barbara enjoying the confidence of an income rider, or Michael balancing growth and security, annuities offer a versatile solution for retirees. By incorporating modern annuity strategies, you can create a retirement plan that ensures financial security and peace of mind for years to come.

In the next chapter, we'll explore how to safeguard your retirement from market volatility, ensuring your income remains steady no matter what happens in the financial world.

Chapter 6: Creating Your Income Plan

Turning your retirement savings into a steady, predictable income is one of the most challenging parts of retirement planning. It's not just about having enough saved; it's about making your money work together, last as long as you need it, and adapt to your changing needs. In this chapter, we'll walk through strategies to create an income plan that fits your life, using the experiences of our six personas as your guide.

The Guaranteed Income Framework

When Susan, the Risk-Averse Safety Seeker, thought about retirement, her biggest fear was outliving her money. "I just need to know my bills are paid every month," she told her advisor. Susan's plan started with guaranteed income sources to cover her essential expenses—housing, utilities, groceries, and healthcare. By combining Social Security with an annuity, Susan built a foundation of stability. This approach let her sleep at night, knowing her basics were always covered.

For Tom, the Near-Retiree Planner, the framework was about preparation. He calculated his essential expenses—$4,000 per month—and identified an income gap of $1,500 after Social Security. Tom worked with a financial professional to secure a Fixed Indexed Annuity that would fill that gap. By doing this before retiring, he ensured his income plan would be ready the day he stopped working.

Creating Your Monthly Paycheck

One of the biggest transitions into retirement is going from receiving a paycheck to creating your own. Barbara, the Recent Retiree Adjuster, struggled with this shift. "I wasn't sure how to turn my savings into monthly income," she admitted. To solve this, Barbara adopted a structured withdrawal strategy:

1. **Start with Guaranteed Income**: Social Security and her annuity formed the base of her monthly paycheck, covering essential expenses.
2. **Add Flexible Income**: Dividend payments and bond interest provided additional funds for discretionary spending.
3. **Supplement as Needed**: When larger expenses came up, Barbara dipped into her growth-oriented accounts, ensuring her withdrawals were intentional and infrequent.
4.

For Margaret, the Long-Lived Optimist, creating a monthly paycheck was essential to maintaining her independence. Her annuity and Social Security combined to provide her with predictable income, while her remaining assets were used sparingly for unexpected expenses. This approach helped her stretch her resources for decades beyond her original retirement plan.

Blending Income Sources

A strong retirement income plan balances guaranteed income, flexible income, and growth potential. Barbara learned this the hard way. In her first year of retirement, a market downturn forced her to sell investments at a loss to pay her bills. To avoid this in the future, Barbara created an income "layering" strategy:

- **Guaranteed Income for Essentials**: Social Security, pension and an annuity covered her housing, food, and healthcare costs.
- **Flexible Income for Lifestyle**: Barbara invested in dividend-paying stocks and bond funds for her discretionary expenses.
- **Growth-Oriented Income for the Future**: She kept part of her savings in a diversified portfolio to outpace inflation.

This blended approach gave Barbara the flexibility to enjoy her retirement without worrying about market swings.

The Income Protection Strategy

Market volatility is a reality retirees can't ignore. David and Lisa, the Established Retiree Optimizers, know this all too well. Early in their retirement, a market downturn forced them to withdraw from their investments at a loss. To protect themselves moving forward, they implemented an income protection strategy:

- **Reserve Fund**: Two years' worth of living expenses in cash and short-term bonds.
- **Guaranteed Income**: An annuity covered their essentials, so they never had to sell investments during a downturn.

- **Risk Management**: Their remaining portfolio was adjusted to align with their risk tolerance, focusing on steady growth rather than aggressive returns.

Michael, the Long-Term Visionary, took a slightly different approach. As someone still in his 50s, he's using a Health Savings Account (HSA) to prepare for future healthcare costs while focusing his investments on tax-efficient growth. "I'm not just planning for income today—I'm thinking about income 20 years from now," he explained. By balancing his priorities, Michael is creating a strategy designed to adapt to life's uncertainties.

The Tax-Smart Withdrawal Strategy

Taxes can erode your retirement income if withdrawals aren't planned carefully. For Michael, reducing taxes is a priority. He strategically converts portions of his traditional IRA to a Roth IRA each year, ensuring he pays taxes now at a lower rate rather than later at potentially higher rates. "*It's about playing the long game*," he says.

David and Lisa also embraced a tax-smart strategy. By coordinating withdrawals from their Roth IRA, taxable accounts, and traditional IRA, they minimized their overall tax burden while maintaining a consistent income. Their advisor helped them structure withdrawals to stay within lower tax brackets and avoid unnecessary penalties.

For Susan, managing taxes meant understanding how Social Security benefits are taxed. She learned to monitor her "combined income" to keep her benefits from being overly taxed. Small adjustments, like taking more withdrawals from her Roth IRA, saved her thousands over time.

Implementation Timeline

Building an income plan takes time and careful execution. Margaret, the Long-Lived Optimist, realized this after outliving her original retirement plan. Her story highlights the importance of starting early and revisiting your strategy regularly. Here's a suggested timeline for implementing your income plan:

- **5-10 Years Before Retirement**: Identify your essential expenses and calculate your income gap. Research annuities or other guaranteed income products.
- **1-2 Years Before Retirement**: Adjust your portfolio to reduce risk. Create a reserve fund for short-term expenses.
- **At Retirement**: Secure your guaranteed income sources. Begin withdrawals from flexible accounts as needed.
- **Throughout Retirement**: Monitor your plan annually. Adjust for inflation, unexpected expenses, or changes in your lifestyle.

Top 3 Items Readers Will Learn:

1. How to blend different income sources (Social Security, annuities, investments) to create a reliable retirement paycheck
2. Strategies for implementing tax-efficient withdrawal plans across different account types
3. Methods for protecting retirement income from market volatility while maintaining growth potential

Creating a reliable retirement income plan isn't just about having enough savings - it's about knowing your money will last no matter what the market does or how long you live. This chapter provides the blueprint for turning your retirement savings into dependable income streams that can support your lifestyle while adapting to changing needs and market conditions.

Chapter 7: Tax-Smart Strategies for Maximizing Your Retirement Income

Taxes don't stop when you retire. In fact, without a solid plan, they can eat away at your hard-earned savings and reduce the longevity of your income. This chapter focuses on strategies to minimize your tax burden and keep more of your money working for you throughout retirement. We'll explore these concepts through the experiences of our six personas, highlighting practical steps and real-life applications.

Understanding Your Tax Landscape

One of the first steps in creating a tax-smart retirement strategy is understanding how taxes apply to various income sources. Social Security, traditional IRAs, Roth IRAs, taxable accounts, and pensions all have unique tax rules. For Michael, the Long-Term Visionary, this understanding started years before retirement. By mapping out his tax situation early, he was able to make informed decisions about Roth conversions and tax-efficient withdrawals.

David and Lisa, the Established Retiree Optimizers, learned this lesson during their first year of retirement. They realized that their combined income from Social Security, pensions, and RMDs pushed them into a higher tax bracket. With the help of their financial advisor, they adjusted their withdrawal strategy to reduce their taxable income and avoid unnecessary penalties.

Understanding Your Tax Brackets

Your tax bracket determines how much of your income is taxed at specific rates, and understanding it is crucial for efficient planning. Barbara, the Recent Retiree Adjuster, learned to track her taxable income carefully. "By staying just under the 22% tax bracket, I saved thousands each year," she shared. Being mindful of how much income pushes you into the next bracket can make a significant difference in your overall tax liability.

The Smart Way to Fill Your Tax Buckets

Tax diversification—spreading your savings across taxable, tax-deferred, and tax-free accounts—provides retirees with flexibility to manage taxes. Tom, the Near-Retiree Planner, worked on creating balanced tax buckets during his working years. In retirement, this allowed him to pull from different accounts strategically. For example, in a year with unexpected expenses, Tom withdrew from his Roth IRA, ensuring his taxable income stayed low while still meeting his needs.

The Roth Conversion Secret

Roth conversions are a powerful way to minimize taxes in retirement. Michael began converting portions of his traditional IRA to a Roth IRA in his 50s. "I viewed it as pre-paying my taxes at a lower rate," he explained. By spreading conversions over several years, he avoided bumping into higher tax brackets and positioned himself for tax-free income in retirement. This strategy worked particularly well during years when his taxable income was lower than expected.

The RMD and IRMAA Challenges

Required Minimum Distributions (RMDs) can create unexpected tax burdens. David and Lisa discovered this when their RMDs increased their taxable income significantly. To address this, they reduced the impact of future RMDs by converting a portion of their IRA to a Roth before RMDs began.

Additionally, higher income can lead to increased Medicare premiums due to Income-Related Monthly Adjustment Amounts (IRMAA). Barbara, aware of this challenge, carefully monitored her income to stay below the IRMAA thresholds, saving her thousands annually on Medicare premiums.

The Social Security Tax Trap

Social Security benefits can be taxed depending on your combined income, which includes your adjusted gross income, non-taxable interest, and half of your Social Security benefits. Susan was surprised to learn that up to 85% of her benefits could be taxable if her income exceeded certain thresholds.

Barbara avoided this by coordinating her withdrawals. By taking more from her Roth IRA and less from her traditional IRA, she stayed below the threshold where her benefits would be heavily taxed. "It's about knowing where your income is coming from," she said.

The Tax-Smart Withdrawal Strategy

Timing is everything when it comes to withdrawals. Margaret, the Long-Lived Optimist, relied heavily on her traditional IRA for years, which increased her taxable income. After working with a financial professional, she shifted to a more tax-efficient strategy:

- **Early Years of Retirement**: Withdraw from taxable accounts first to minimize capital gains taxes.
- **Before RMDs Begin**: Use this period for Roth conversions or withdrawals from traditional IRAs to reduce future RMDs.
- **After RMDs Start**: Coordinate withdrawals to stay within a manageable tax bracket.

David and Lisa took a similar approach, using their early retirement years to convert a significant portion of their IRA funds into a Roth. This allowed them to reduce the impact of RMDs and keep their taxes predictable.

Actionable Steps for Tax-Smart Strategies

1. **Map Out Your Taxable Income**: Understand how each income source contributes to your tax liability.
2. **Explore Roth Conversions**: Start small and spread conversions over several years to minimize tax impact.
3. **Coordinate Withdrawals**: Use a strategic order to draw from taxable, tax-deferred, and tax-free accounts.

4. **Monitor Tax Brackets**: Stay aware of how your income impacts your tax bracket and adjust withdrawals accordingly.
5. **Plan for RMDs and IRMAA**: Prepare for these challenges early to avoid surprise costs.
6. **Seek Professional Guidance**: Work with a tax advisor or financial planner to tailor strategies to your unique situation.

Top 3 Items Readers Will Learn:

1. How to coordinate withdrawals from different account types (Traditional, Roth, taxable) to minimize taxes
2. Strategies for managing RMDs and their tax impact through advance planning
3. Methods to avoid or minimize Social Security benefit taxation through income planning

It's not just how much you save for retirement that matters - it's how much you keep after taxes that determines your lifestyle. By implementing the tax-smart strategies outlined in this chapter, you can potentially save thousands in unnecessary taxes and significantly increase your spendable retirement income.

Bringing It All Together

Taxes don't have to be a retirement drain. With proactive planning, you can minimize your tax burden and maximize the longevity of your income. Whether it's Michael's long-term vision, Susan's adjustments to avoid Social Security taxes, or David and Lisa's strategic use of Roth conversions, these strategies prove that small changes can lead to big results.

In the next chapter, we'll discuss strategies for protecting your retirement assets from market volatility, ensuring your income remains steady no matter what happens in the financial world.

Reference our other book "12 Smart Tax Strategies for Retirees" for more information on how to save taxes in retirement.

In the next chapter, we'll discuss strategies for protecting your retirement assets from market volatility, ensuring your income remains steady no matter what happens in the financial world.

Reference our other book "The Smart Tax Strategies for Retirees" for more information on how to save taxes in retirement.

Chapter 8: Protecting Your Retirement

Retirement planning isn't just about saving and spending; it's about safeguarding your future against the inevitable risks that come with aging, health, and legacy planning. This chapter dives into the essential strategies for protecting your retirement, touching on healthcare, long-term care, estate planning, and how to ensure your family is prepared for the future. Let's explore these critical topics in detail.

Healthcare Planning Essentials

Healthcare expenses are one of the biggest financial concerns for retirees. For Susan, the Risk-Averse Safety Seeker, the fear of unexpected medical bills was a significant stressor. She knew Medicare would help, but she also understood it wouldn't cover everything.

A solid healthcare plan begins with understanding your potential costs. On average, a 65-year-old couple retiring today can expect to spend over $315,000 on healthcare during retirement. This includes premiums, out-of-pocket expenses, and long-term care. Planning for these costs is as much about peace of mind as it is about financial stability.

Michael, the Long-Term Visionary, took proactive steps by contributing to a Health Savings Account (HSA) while he was still working. By maxing out his contributions and investing the funds, he created a tax-free reserve specifically for medical expenses. For him, this strategy was not just a safety net but a tool for growth.

It's also vital to compare Medicare Supplement (Medigap) plans or Medicare Advantage plans. Barbara, the Recent Retiree Adjuster, chose a Medigap plan to minimize her out-of-pocket costs. The key is selecting a plan that aligns with your expected healthcare needs, including prescriptions and routine care.

The Medicare Decision

Medicare is a cornerstone of healthcare in retirement, but navigating its complexities can be daunting. David and Lisa, the Established Retiree Optimizers, spent hours researching their options. They learned that enrolling on time is crucial to avoid late penalties and gaps in coverage. Medicare has four parts: Part A (hospital insurance), Part B (medical insurance), Part C (Medicare Advantage), and Part D (prescription drug coverage). Susan opted for original Medicare combined with a Medigap plan to cover gaps. Meanwhile, Michael chose a Medicare Advantage plan because it included additional benefits like vision and dental coverage.

The decision doesn't end with choosing a plan. Each year during open enrollment, retirees should reassess their needs and ensure their current plan still fits. For Margaret, the Long-Lived Optimist, this annual review saved her hundreds by switching Part D plans to better suit her changing prescriptions.

The Drug Coverage Gap

Prescription drug costs are another major concern. The infamous "donut hole" in Medicare Part D coverage leaves many retirees with unexpected expenses. Barbara was shocked to find herself in the coverage gap after her medication costs exceeded $4,660 in a single year.

To mitigate this, Barbara researched generic alternatives and used mail-order services to reduce costs. Michael, always forward-thinking, also explored pharmaceutical assistance programs offered by manufacturers. Knowing your options and being proactive can significantly reduce out-of-pocket expenses.

For David and Lisa, choosing a Part D plan that included comprehensive coverage for their most expensive medications was a priority. They used Medicare's online plan finder to compare costs and benefits across multiple providers.

The Long-Term Care Insurance Versus Long-Term Care Annuities

Long-term care is one of the most unpredictable and expensive aspects of retirement. Barbara, who purchased long-term care insurance in her late 50s, was relieved to know she'd have coverage if she needed assisted living or in-home care.

David and Lisa, however, opted for a hybrid approach. They purchased a long-term care annuity with a rider for additional coverage. This gave them guaranteed income and the flexibility to use funds for care if needed.
For Susan, who preferred to avoid traditional insurance, self-insuring through careful savings and investments was her strategy. Each approach has its merits, and choosing the right one depends on your health, risk tolerance, and financial goals.

Understanding Your Options

The key to successful long-term care planning is understanding your options. Traditional insurance policies provide robust coverage but can be costly and subject to premium increases. Hybrid products, like annuities or life insurance with long-term care riders, offer more flexibility. Margaret, who's now 92, regrets not planning earlier. Her experience highlights the importance of addressing long-term care while you're still healthy enough to qualify for favorable terms. For her, leveraging home equity became a last-resort option to cover care costs.

The Self-Insurance Strategy

Some retirees, like Michael, prefer to self-insure. By setting aside a dedicated portion of savings for future care, they avoid paying premiums for insurance they may never use. Michael's strategy included keeping these funds in low-risk, high-liquidity investments to ensure they're available when needed.

However, self-insurance isn't without risk. Unexpected medical costs can quickly deplete these reserves. Barbara's advice is to have a backup plan, such as leveraging other assets or a reverse mortgage, to cover unexpected gaps.

Using Life Insurance Strategically

Modern life insurance products are versatile tools for retirement planning. Susan used a cash-value life insurance policy to supplement her retirement income while maintaining a death benefit for her heirs. "*It's nice to know I'm protected, but I also have flexibility*," she said.

Hybrid policies that combine life insurance with long-term care benefits are gaining popularity. David and Lisa chose this option, ensuring they had funds for care if needed and leaving a legacy if not. For them, it was a win-win solution.

The New Life Insurance Options

Today's life insurance policies go beyond traditional death benefits. Features like accelerated death benefits, long-term care riders, and cash value growth make these products more than just safety nets.

Michael researched indexed universal life (IUL) policies to add tax-advantaged growth to his retirement plan. For him, the ability to borrow against the policy's cash value provided an additional layer of financial security.

Estate Planning Fundamentals

Estate planning is not just for the ultra-wealthy; it's for anyone who wants to ensure their wishes are honored and their assets distributed efficiently. Barbara, the Recent Retiree Adjuster, started with a simple will but quickly realized she needed a more comprehensive plan to protect her family's future.

A robust estate plan includes more than just a will. It considers tax implications, healthcare directives, and the unique needs of your beneficiaries. For example, David and Lisa, the Established Retiree Optimizers, used a combination of trusts and beneficiary designations to streamline the process and avoid probate. "We wanted to make things as simple as possible for our kids," Lisa said.

Proper estate planning also accounts for digital assets. Margaret, the Long-Lived Optimist, created a digital inventory of her online accounts to ensure her executor could access them. Estate planning is an ongoing process that requires regular updates to reflect life changes such as new family members, divorces, or significant financial events.

Beyond the Basic Will

A will is a foundational element of any estate plan, but it's often not enough to cover all your needs. Susan, the Risk-Averse Safety Seeker, initially thought a will would suffice, but her attorney explained the benefits of adding a living trust. A trust not only avoids probate but also ensures privacy and immediate access to assets upon her passing.

David and Lisa included a special needs trust in their plan to protect a disabled family member's inheritance without jeopardizing government benefits. "We didn't want our good intentions to unintentionally cause harm," David explained. These additional steps go beyond a basic will, providing layers of protection tailored to unique family situations.

The Power of Powers

Assigning power of attorney is one of the most critical steps in estate planning. Margaret learned this the hard way when she fell ill and her children struggled to access her financial accounts. By designating a financial and healthcare power of attorney, you ensure that someone you trust can make decisions on your behalf if you become incapacitated.

Michael, the Long-Term Visionary, added a durable power of attorney to his estate plan. "I wanted to be proactive so my family isn't scrambling if something happens," he said. Choosing the right person is key; this individual will have significant control over your finances and healthcare decisions.

Protecting Your Healthcare Wishes

Healthcare decisions can be emotionally and financially draining for families, especially without clear guidance. Barbara worked with her attorney to draft an advance directive and a living will. These documents outlined her preferences for end-of-life care, ensuring her family wouldn't have to make difficult decisions under stress.

David and Lisa included a healthcare proxy in their estate plan. "We trust each other to make the right decisions if one of us can't," Lisa said. Advance healthcare planning gives you peace of mind knowing your wishes will be respected while sparing your family unnecessary heartache.

The Trust Decision

Trusts are powerful tools for estate planning, offering benefits like avoiding probate, protecting assets, and reducing estate taxes. Michael created a revocable living trust to streamline asset management while maintaining control during his lifetime. "It's like having a financial safety net," he said.

For families with complex needs, such as blended families or substantial assets, trusts can offer additional layers of protection. Margaret's trust ensured her grandchildren's education would be funded without risking their financial aid eligibility. Trusts are not one-size-fits-all; consult with an estate planning professional to tailor them to your situation.

Protecting Your Passwords

In today's digital world, securing online accounts is an essential part of estate planning. Barbara compiled a master list of her passwords and stored it securely, ensuring her executor could access important financial accounts and digital assets. "It's one less thing for my family to worry about," she said.

Digital estate planning should include social media accounts, email, and any online subscriptions. Using a password manager can simplify the process and ensure your digital life is organized and accessible.

The IRA Inheritance Trap

IRA inheritance rules can be complex, especially with changes to the Stretch IRA provisions. David and Lisa worked closely with their advisor to educate their children about required minimum distributions (RMDs) and how to avoid costly tax mistakes.

Michael designated his Roth IRA to his spouse to ensure tax-free inheritance. For non-spouse beneficiaries, understanding the 10-year rule for IRA distributions is crucial to avoiding penalties. Proper planning can prevent your heirs from being hit with an unexpected tax bill.

Making Your Protection Plan Work

Creating a comprehensive estate plan is only half the battle; ensuring it works when needed is equally important. Margaret organized a master file containing her will, trust documents, insurance policies, and account statements. She also included instructions for her executor, making the transition seamless for her family.

Creating Your Master File

A master file is a centralized location for all essential documents, including:

- Your will and trusts
- Powers of attorney
- Healthcare directives
- Insurance policies
- Account statements

David and Lisa shared their master file with their children during a family meeting, ensuring everyone knew where to find important information.

The Family Meeting

Communication is key to avoiding misunderstandings. Barbara held a family meeting to discuss her estate plan, answering questions and addressing concerns. "It brought us closer as a family," she said. These meetings ensure everyone is on the same page and reduces the risk of conflict later.

Small Changes, Big Impact

Sometimes, minor adjustments can have significant effects. Susan updated her beneficiary designations, avoiding probate for certain accounts and saving her family time and money. Regularly reviewing your estate plan ensures it remains aligned with your goals.

Your Action Steps

- Review your estate plan annually to account for changes in your life or the law.
- Organize a master file with all critical documents.

- Communicate your plan to your family through a meeting or written instructions.

Protecting your retirement is an ongoing process that ensures your financial and personal legacy. With thoughtful planning, you can safeguard your future and provide peace of mind for your loved ones.

Top 3 Items Readers Will Learn:

1. How to navigate Medicare decisions and supplement coverage gaps
2. Strategies for addressing long-term care risks through insurance, self-funding, or hybrid approaches
3. Essential estate planning steps including wills, trusts, powers of attorney, and digital asset protection

Having a secure retirement isn't just about having enough money - it's about protecting yourself and your loved ones from the unexpected events that could derail your financial security. This chapter provides the roadmap for putting proper protections in place, giving you peace of mind that your retirement plan can withstand healthcare challenges, long-term care needs, and ensure your legacy wishes are fulfilled.

Bringing It All Together

Protecting your retirement is more than just a financial exercise; it's a way to ensure your legacy is preserved and your loved ones are spared unnecessary hardship. By addressing each of the topics discussed in this chapter—estate planning, healthcare wishes, trusts, and family communication—you build a solid foundation of security and peace of mind.

The stories of Barbara, David and Lisa, Michael, and Margaret demonstrate that while the specifics of protection planning vary for everyone, the principles remain universal: plan early, communicate openly, and revisit your strategies regularly. A well-crafted plan is your best defense against the uncertainties of life and ensures your values and priorities are carried forward.

Looking Ahead

In the next chapter, we'll explore how to maintain flexibility and adapt your retirement strategies as life evolves. Retirement isn't static; your plans need to account for changing circumstances, new opportunities, and unforeseen challenges. By staying proactive, you can continue to enjoy a fulfilling and secure retirement.

Chapter 9 Investment Strategies That Work

Investing in retirement requires a different mindset than during your working years. The stakes are higher, and the goals shift from growth to generating income while preserving what you've worked so hard to save. This chapter will explore the new rules of portfolio income, the three-bucket strategy, and proven ways to make your money last through your retirement years.

The New Rules of Portfolio Income

Gone are the days when a simple 4% withdrawal rule guaranteed a worry-free retirement. Market volatility, rising life expectancies, and low-interest rates have reshaped how retirees should think about portfolio income. Barbara, the Recent Retiree Adjuster, learned this the hard way. In her first year of retirement, a significant market downturn forced her to withdraw from her investments at a loss, jeopardizing her long-term financial stability.

Today's retirees must adopt more dynamic withdrawal strategies. One approach is the "guardrails" method, where withdrawal rates are adjusted based on portfolio performance. For instance, during strong market years, retirees might take slightly more income, while reducing withdrawals during down markets helps preserve the portfolio.

Michael, the Long-Term Visionary, combines a diversified portfolio with guaranteed income products. "It's about balancing risk and reward," he said. By blending annuities, Social Security, and a portfolio designed for growth, Michael ensures that his essential expenses are covered while still allowing room for discretionary spending.

Tax efficiency is another critical component. Susan, the Risk-Averse Safety Seeker, discovered that withdrawing strategically from her taxable, tax-deferred, and Roth accounts minimized her tax burden, allowing her to keep more of her money working for her.

The Three-Bucket Strategy

The three-bucket strategy is a simple yet effective way to manage retirement income by dividing your assets into short-term, mid-term, and long-term buckets. David and Lisa, the Established Retiree Optimizers, implemented this approach to create a clear plan for their spending needs.

1. **Short-Term Bucket**: This bucket covers immediate expenses for the next 1-3 years. It's made up of cash and cash equivalents like money market accounts. Barbara's short-term bucket includes enough to cover her essential living expenses, so she doesn't need to worry about market fluctuations.

2. **Mid-Term Bucket**: Designed for spending needs over the next 4-10 years, this bucket typically includes bonds and other income-generating assets. Margaret, the Long-Lived Optimist, keeps her mid-term bucket in high-quality corporate bonds, providing steady income without taking on excessive risk.

3. **Long-Term Bucket**: This bucket focuses on growth and is meant for expenses 10 or more years down the road. It includes stocks, mutual funds, or ETFs. Michael's long-term bucket is heavily invested in equities, ensuring that his portfolio keeps pace with inflation and supports his lifestyle well into his later years.

4.

The key to the three-bucket strategy is regular rebalancing. David and Lisa review their buckets annually, replenishing their short-term bucket from the mid-term bucket and rebalancing their long-term investments based on market performance.

Making Your Money Last

Longevity is both a blessing and a challenge. Margaret's story highlights this reality. At 92, she's been retired for nearly 30 years, far longer than she initially planned. Ensuring your money lasts requires a combination of smart planning, flexibility, and discipline.

One effective strategy is to build an income floor using guaranteed income sources. For Susan, this includes Social Security and an annuity that covers her basic living expenses. "Knowing my essentials are covered gives me peace of mind," she explained.

Another approach is to embrace partial withdrawals rather than relying solely on portfolio income. Michael maintains a portion of his portfolio in a Roth IRA, allowing him to take tax-free withdrawals when needed, preserving the rest of his assets.

Flexibility is also crucial. Barbara adjusted her spending habits during a market downturn, cutting discretionary expenses like travel to avoid dipping into her long-term savings. "*It's about being adaptable*," she said.

To make your money last, consider these actionable steps:

- **Diversify Your Income Sources**: Blend Social Security, annuities, and portfolio withdrawals for stability.
- **Plan for Inflation**: Include growth-oriented investments to keep up with rising costs.
- **Manage Your Withdrawals**: Stick to a flexible withdrawal strategy that adapts to market conditions.
- **Consult a Professional**: Work with a financial advisor to tailor strategies to your unique needs.

The Dividend Growth Strategy

The dividend growth strategy focuses on investing in companies that consistently increase their dividend payouts over time. This approach is especially appealing to retirees looking for a reliable income stream that can keep pace with inflation. Michael, the Long-Term Visionary, began incorporating dividend growth stocks into his portfolio in his late 50s, recognizing their potential for both income and capital appreciation. "I wanted income I could count on, but I also wanted it to grow," he explained.

Dividend growth investing is not just about picking high-yield stocks; it's about selecting companies with strong fundamentals and a history of increasing dividends. These companies often operate in stable industries, such as utilities, consumer staples, and healthcare, making them less susceptible to economic downturns. Barbara, the Recent Retiree Adjuster, allocated a portion of her portfolio to dividend growth stocks after realizing their ability to provide steady income without relying solely on market appreciation.

One of the key benefits of this strategy is its compounding effect. By reinvesting dividends during your pre-retirement years, you can significantly boost your total returns. For Susan, the Risk-Averse Safety Seeker, this meant allowing her dividends to accumulate and purchase additional shares automatically, creating a snowball effect that increased her income over time.

However, dividend growth investing requires careful selection and monitoring. Not all companies with high yields are good investments. Some may have unsustainable payout ratios, meaning they distribute more in dividends than they earn, which can lead to cuts or eliminations. Margaret, the Long-Lived Optimist, learned this lesson early and now ensures she diversifies her dividend holdings across multiple sectors and geographies.

When building a dividend growth portfolio, consider these factors:

- **Dividend Growth Rate**: Look for companies with a history of increasing their dividends annually.

- **Payout Ratio**: A healthy payout ratio (typically below 60%) indicates the company can sustain and grow its dividend.
- **Financial Health**: Focus on companies with strong balance sheets and stable cash flows.
- **Sector Diversification**: Avoid over-concentrating in one sector to reduce risk.

The dividend growth strategy is not a one-size-fits-all solution, but it offers a compelling way to generate reliable income while preserving and potentially growing your capital. As Michael put it, "*It's about finding that sweet spot where income meets growth.*"

Building Your Dividend Portfolio

Building a dividend portfolio isn't just about picking the highest-yielding stocks; it's about creating a balanced, diversified collection of investments that can provide consistent income while growing over time. Michael, the Long-Term Visionary, started by identifying companies with a strong history of dividend growth. "I wanted a portfolio that could sustain me for decades," he said, emphasizing the importance of sustainability and long-term planning.

To start, focus on companies with a history of paying and increasing dividends. These companies are often referred to as "Dividend Aristocrats"—companies that have increased their dividends for at least 25 consecutive years. Susan, the Risk-Averse Safety Seeker, prioritized these types of companies in sectors like utilities, healthcare, and consumer staples. She appreciated their stability and the likelihood that they would continue to perform well even during economic downturns.

Diversification is key to mitigating risk. Margaret, the Long-Lived Optimist, ensures her portfolio spans multiple industries and regions. "I don't want all my income tied to one sector," she explained. By investing in a mix of domestic and international stocks, Margaret protects her portfolio from localized economic issues while benefiting from global growth opportunities.

When selecting stocks, consider the payout ratio—the percentage of earnings a company pays out as dividends. A lower payout ratio (generally below 60%) indicates that a company has room to grow its dividend even in tough times. Barbara, the Recent Retiree Adjuster, learned to avoid stocks with excessively high payout ratios, as they often signal potential financial strain for the company.

In addition to individual stocks, exchange-traded funds (ETFs) and mutual funds focused on dividends can provide instant diversification. These funds pool investments in dividend-paying companies, making them an excellent choice for retirees who prefer a hands-off approach. David and Lisa, the Established Retiree Optimizers, included a dividend ETF in their portfolio to complement their individual stock holdings.

When building your portfolio, remember these tips:

- **Start with Quality**: Focus on companies with a proven track record of dividend growth.
- **Diversify**: Spread your investments across sectors and regions to reduce risk.
- **Monitor Regularly**: Revisit your portfolio annually to ensure it aligns with your income needs and market conditions.

- **Reinvest When Possible**: If you're still in your pre-retirement years, reinvest dividends to benefit from compounding.

A well-constructed dividend portfolio can be a cornerstone of your retirement strategy, providing reliable income and the potential for growth. As Barbara noted, "*It's comforting to know my portfolio is working for me, even when the markets are unpredictable.*"

The Safe Withdrawal Strategy

The safe withdrawal strategy is a cornerstone of retirement planning, ensuring you can draw from your savings without running out of money. It's about balancing your need for income with the need to preserve your principal. Barbara, the Recent Retiree Adjuster, initially followed the traditional 4% rule but quickly realized it needed to be adjusted for market volatility and her own spending patterns.

The 4% rule, a long-standing guideline, suggests withdrawing 4% of your portfolio in the first year of retirement and adjusting for inflation each subsequent year. While it's a useful starting point, it's not a one-size-fits-all solution. Michael, the Long-Term Visionary, prefers a more dynamic approach, adjusting his withdrawals based on market performance. "When the market does well, I might take a bit more, but in down years, I scale back," he explained.

A key component of a safe withdrawal strategy is diversification. David and Lisa, the Established Retiree Optimizers, structured their portfolio with a mix of stocks, bonds, and guaranteed income products. This allowed them to weather market downturns without having to sell investments at a loss. Their approach provides stability and ensures their income needs are met regardless of market conditions.

Flexibility is another critical factor. Margaret, the Long-Lived Optimist, adapts her spending to her portfolio's performance. "I've learned to cut back on discretionary expenses during lean years," she shared. This adaptability has helped her stretch her savings for decades, providing her with financial security even into her 90s.

For those looking to implement a safe withdrawal strategy, consider these tips:

- **Start with a Baseline**: Use the 4% rule as a starting point but be prepared to adjust.
- **Diversify Your Portfolio**: A mix of asset classes can reduce risk and provide more stable returns.
- **Be Flexible**: Adapt your spending to market conditions to preserve your savings.
- **Use Guardrails**: Establish upper and lower limits on withdrawals to prevent overspending or unnecessary frugality.

The safe withdrawal strategy is not about rigid rules; it's about creating a sustainable income plan that adapts to your life and the markets. As Michael wisely put it, "The goal is to make your money last as long as you do, without sacrificing the quality of your retirement."

Making Bonds Work Today

Bonds have long been considered a cornerstone of retirement portfolios, providing stability and income. However, in today's low-interest-rate environment, making bonds work effectively requires a more strategic approach. Michael, the Long-Term Visionary, emphasizes, *"You can't just rely on bonds the way our parents did; you have to be smart about where you invest."*

One way to enhance bond performance is through diversification. This doesn't just mean holding a mix of corporate and government bonds but also considering global bonds, inflation-protected securities, and high-yield bonds. Barbara, the Recent Retiree Adjuster, added Treasury Inflation-Protected Securities (TIPS) to her portfolio to guard against rising costs. "I wanted to make sure my income wouldn't lose value over time," she explained.

Another strategy is to create a bond ladder. This involves purchasing bonds with staggered maturity dates to ensure a steady stream of income and the ability to reinvest as each bond matures. David and Lisa, the Established Retiree Optimizers, found that a five-year bond ladder provided them with reliable cash flow while reducing the risk of being locked into low rates for too long.

Investors must also pay attention to credit quality. High-yield bonds offer attractive returns but come with increased risk. Margaret, the Long-Lived Optimist, balances her portfolio by holding a mix of investment-grade corporate bonds and municipal bonds. Municipal bonds are particularly appealing because of their tax advantages, which can be a boon for retirees in higher tax brackets.

Interest rate sensitivity is another critical factor. When rates rise, bond prices typically fall. Susan, the Risk-Averse Safety Seeker, mitigates this risk by keeping the duration of her bond portfolio short to intermediate. "It's about staying nimble and protecting my principal," she said.

To make bonds work for you, consider these actionable steps:

- **Diversify Bond Types**: Include corporate, government, and municipal bonds, as well as global options.
- **Build a Ladder**: Create a bond ladder to ensure steady income and reinvestment opportunities.
- **Focus on Quality**: Prioritize investment-grade bonds for stability.
- **Be Mindful of Duration**: Adjust the duration of your portfolio to align with interest rate trends.

While bonds may not offer the same returns they once did, they remain a vital component of a well-rounded retirement portfolio. As Michael wisely noted, "*Bonds are about stability, and in retirement, stability is priceless.*"

Real Estate Rental Income: A Reliable Source of Retirement Cash Flow

Real estate rental income can be a powerful addition to your retirement strategy. Owning rental properties not only provides a steady income stream but also offers potential tax advantages and long-term asset growth. Unlike more volatile investment vehicles, real estate income is typically stable and predictable, making it a favored choice for retirees seeking financial security.

The Benefits of Rental Income

Rental income provides multiple advantages for retirees:

- **Predictable Cash Flow**: Monthly rental payments can act as a consistent income source, helping cover living expenses or fund discretionary spending.
- **Inflation Hedge**: Property values and rental rates tend to rise over time, protecting your income against inflation.
- **Tax Benefits**: Real estate owners can take advantage of deductions for expenses like property management, maintenance, and depreciation, effectively reducing taxable income.

For Barbara, a recent retiree seeking to stabilize her finances, owning a rental property became a critical component of her income strategy. "It's reassuring to know that I have a predictable check coming in every month," she says.

Building Your Portfolio

Investing in rental properties requires careful planning and due diligence. When considering rental real estate, keep these factors in mind:

1. **Location**: Choose areas with high demand for rentals, such as neighborhoods near schools, hospitals, or major employers.
2. **Type of Property**: Single-family homes, multifamily units, or vacation rentals each come with unique advantages and challenges.
3. **Cash Flow Potential**: Ensure that rental income exceeds expenses, including mortgage payments, taxes, insurance, and maintenance.

David and Lisa, seasoned retirees with rental properties, emphasize the importance of property management. "We didn't want the hassle of managing tenants ourselves, so we hired a property manager to handle the day-to-day tasks," Lisa explains.

The Risks to Consider

While rental income offers stability, it's not without risks. Vacancies, unexpected repairs, and fluctuations in property values can impact your bottom line. To mitigate these risks:

- Maintain an emergency fund for unexpected expenses. A money market or high yield savings account is a good place to keep this money.
- Regularly inspect and maintain your properties to prevent costly repairs.
- Diversify your investments by avoiding over-reliance on rental income.

Michael, a forward-thinking investor, uses rental income to fund his Roth IRA contributions, ensuring his retirement income remains diversified. "It's all about balance," he notes.

Is Real Estate Right for You?

Real estate rental income isn't for everyone. Managing properties can be time-consuming and stressful, especially for retirees who prefer a more hands-off approach. If this is a concern, consider alternative options like real estate investment trusts (REITs), which provide the benefits of real estate investing without the responsibilities of property management.

For Susan, a cautious retiree, REITs were a better fit. "I wanted the stability of real estate without the headaches," she shares. By investing in REITs, she diversified her portfolio while enjoying the income and growth potential of the real estate market.

Taking the Next Step

Real estate rental income can play a vital role in your retirement plan, providing consistent cash flow and long-term security. Whether you're ready to purchase your first property or exploring passive investment options like REITs, the key is to align your real estate strategy with your overall retirement goals.

By following a well-thought-out plan and seeking professional advice, you can unlock the full potential of real estate rental income and enjoy a more financially secure retirement.

The Inflation Fighter Strategy

Inflation can silently erode the purchasing power of your retirement income over time, making it one of the most insidious threats to long-term financial security. To counter this, the Inflation Fighter Strategy focuses on incorporating assets and income streams that grow alongside or outpace inflation. This approach ensures your retirement savings maintain their value, even as costs rise.

Key Components of the Inflation Fighter Strategy

A well-rounded Inflation Fighter Strategy might include the following elements:

- **Growth-Oriented Investments**: Allocating a portion of your portfolio to equities or equity-based funds can provide the long-term growth necessary to keep pace with inflation.
- **Inflation-Protected Securities**: Treasury Inflation-Protected Securities (TIPS) adjust their principal value based on inflation rates, offering a direct hedge against rising costs.
- **Fixed Indexed Annuities with Inflation Riders**: These annuities can provide guaranteed income with adjustments tied to inflation, ensuring your purchasing power remains intact.

For David and Lisa, retirees in their mid-70s, combining TIPS with a Fixed Indexed Annuity provided a solid inflation hedge. "We sleep better knowing our income grows as our expenses do," Lisa shared.

Balancing Risk and Reward

While combating inflation, it's important to balance the potential for growth with the need to protect your principal. Diversification across asset classes, including bonds, stocks, and inflation-protected instruments, reduces overall risk. Retirees often prioritize a combination of safety and growth, creating a sustainable portfolio that meets both short- and long-term needs.

Margaret, a retiree in her 80s, relies on dividend-paying stocks to provide both income and growth. "The dividends help cover my expenses, and the value of my investments grows, keeping me ahead of inflation," she said.

Actionable Steps

To implement the Inflation Fighter Strategy, consider these steps:

1. **Assess Your Expenses**: Identify which costs are most likely to rise with inflation, such as healthcare and utilities.
2. **Allocate for Growth**: Invest in equities, real estate, or other growth-oriented assets that historically outpace inflation.
3. **Incorporate Inflation-Linked Products**: Use tools like TIPS or annuities with inflation riders to add stability to your plan.
4. **Monitor and Adjust**: Regularly review your portfolio to ensure it aligns with current inflation trends and your financial goals.

Real-Life Application

Susan, a cautious retiree, found that adding a mix of TIPS and a small portion of her portfolio in growth stocks provided the confidence to face rising living costs. "Knowing my income is protected gives me the freedom to enjoy retirement," she explained.

The Inflation Fighter Strategy is about more than just investments—it's about peace of mind. By addressing inflation head-on, you can ensure your retirement income keeps pace with the world around you, securing your lifestyle for years to come.

Top 3 Items Readers Will Learn:

1. How to implement the three-bucket strategy for balancing short-term needs with long-term growth
2. Methods for building a sustainable dividend portfolio for reliable retirement income
3. Strategies for making bonds work effectively in a challenging interest rate environment

Successful retirement investing isn't about maximizing returns - it's about creating reliable income while protecting against risks that could derail your retirement. The strategies outlined in this chapter show you how to build an investment portfolio that can provide both the income you need today and the growth you'll need tomorrow, regardless of market conditions.

Bring it together

Investment strategies in retirement must address a balance of growth, stability, and income. From the Three-Bucket Strategy to the Inflation Fighter Strategy, each approach plays a vital role in securing your financial future. Retirement planning isn't about chasing returns; it's about creating a sustainable plan that aligns with your goals, risk tolerance, and lifestyle.

By diversifying income sources, managing withdrawal strategies, and incorporating tools like TIPS, dividend growth stocks, and annuities, you can build a retirement portfolio designed to weather market volatility and inflation. The key is flexibility—adjusting your strategies as economic conditions and personal circumstances change.

Retirees like David and Lisa, who combine steady income with growth-oriented investments, and Michael, who carefully balances risk and reward, demonstrate the power of thoughtful planning. These strategies ensure not only a secure retirement but also the ability to adapt and thrive in the face of uncertainties.

Now that you've learned how to structure your investments to support your retirement, the next step is to put all the pieces together. A plan is only as good as its execution, and having a clear roadmap for implementation is essential.

Chapter 10: Your Implementation Blueprint

Retirement planning is not a one-size-fits-all process. It's a personalized journey that requires careful consideration of your goals, resources, and unique challenges. In this chapter, we'll guide you through creating an actionable implementation blueprint that turns the strategies discussed in this book into a comprehensive retirement plan.

From identifying your priorities to executing key financial decisions, your blueprint will help you navigate every aspect of retirement planning with confidence. We'll explore topics such as:

- Setting realistic goals and timelines
- Integrating income, investment, and tax strategies
- Monitoring and adjusting your plan over time
- Leveraging professional resources for guidance

By the end of this chapter, you'll have a clear path forward, equipped with the tools and insights needed to create a retirement plan that grows with you. Let's turn your vision of a secure and fulfilling retirement into reality.

Starting With What Matters Most

When planning for retirement, it's essential to focus on what truly matters: creating a foundation that supports your goals and priorities. Retirement isn't one-size-fits-all, and the first step is to align your plan with your unique needs and lifestyle aspirations. For many retirees, this means understanding their essential expenses and ensuring they are covered by guaranteed income sources like Social Security, pensions, and annuities.

The Near-Retiree Planner

For Tom, the 58-year-old engineer preparing to retire in seven years, starting with what matters most meant identifying his essential expenses. By working with a financial professional, he created a budget that accounted for housing, healthcare, and utilities. He realized his Social Security would cover about 60% of these costs, leaving a gap he needed to address. To fill it, Tom began exploring Fixed Indexed Annuities to provide additional guaranteed income.

The Recent Retiree Adjuster

Barbara, a 63-year-old who retired two years ago, had underestimated her essential expenses when she first stopped working. Initially, she assumed she'd need only 70% of her working income but soon found that healthcare costs and travel were higher than expected. By revisiting her plan, Barbara adjusted her budget and shifted some of her investments into income-generating assets to ensure her essential expenses were always covered.

The Established Retiree Optimizers

David and Lisa, retirees in their early 70s, focused on optimizing their existing plan. They had covered their essential expenses with Social Security and a small pension but were looking to refine their strategy. By calculating their exact income needs and reviewing their discretionary spending, they reallocated a portion of their portfolio to dividend-paying stocks and inflation-protected securities to guard against rising costs.

The Risk-Averse Safety Seeker

For Susan, a 66-year-old widow, security was paramount. She prioritized covering her essential expenses through guaranteed income sources, ensuring she wouldn't have to worry about market fluctuations. By working with a retirement advisor, Susan used a portion of her savings to purchase an annuity that provided a steady income stream to complement her Social Security benefits.

The Long-Term Visionary

Michael, a 54-year-old business owner, took a proactive approach to planning for his future. For him, starting with what mattered most was about minimizing future tax burdens while building a sustainable income plan. He began converting portions of his traditional IRA to a Roth IRA and invested in a mix of growth-oriented assets and inflation-protected securities to ensure his essential expenses would be covered for decades to come.

The Long-Lived Optimist

At 92, Margaret's retirement had lasted far longer than she initially planned. For her, starting with what matters most meant adjusting to new realities. By tracking her expenses and working with her family, she used home equity and her remaining savings to maintain her lifestyle. Margaret's experience highlighted the importance of reviewing and adapting plans as life evolves.

Actionable Steps

Starting with what matters most is about building a secure foundation for your retirement. Here's how each persona approached the first steps:

1. **Identify Essential Expenses**: Include housing, food, insurance, and healthcare costs.
2. **Calculate Guaranteed Income**: Add up reliable sources like Social Security and pensions.
3. **Address Gaps**: Use annuities, Roth conversions, or growth-oriented assets to cover any shortfall.
4. **Adjust as Needed**: Regularly revisit your plan to reflect changing circumstances and goals.

By focusing on what matters most, you can create a retirement plan that not only meets your financial needs but also aligns with your values and aspirations. Whether you're a near-retiree or decades into retirement, starting with the essentials sets the stage for a secure and fulfilling future.

Building Your Income Stream

Turning retirement savings into a consistent income stream is one of the most critical and challenging aspects of retirement planning. It's not just about having enough money saved—it's about making your funds last and adapt to your needs over time. Creating a sustainable income stream involves a thoughtful blend of guaranteed income, flexible withdrawals, and growth-oriented investments.

Tom and Barbara's Retirement Paycheck

Tom and Barbara, the Near-Retiree Planner and the Recent Retiree Adjuster, wanted their retirement income to feel like a regular paycheck. To achieve this, they started by setting up automatic deposits of their Social Security and pension payments. Then, they addressed their income gaps with a Fixed Indexed Annuity, ensuring they had predictable and guaranteed payments for life. Finally, they structured their investments to provide additional monthly income for discretionary expenses.

Barbara noted, "It's like we created our own pension. It gives us peace of mind knowing our essentials are always covered." Their experience demonstrates how combining different income sources can provide both security and flexibility in retirement.

Balancing Flexibility and Stability

For Susan, the Risk-Averse Safety Seeker, the focus was on stability. She relied heavily on guaranteed income sources, such as Social Security and an annuity, to cover her essential expenses. This foundation allowed her to enjoy discretionary spending without worrying about market volatility.

On the other hand, Michael, the Long-Term Visionary, took a more balanced approach. By incorporating dividend-paying stocks and a Roth IRA into his plan, he ensured that his income could grow and adapt over time. "I wanted reliable income for today but also room for growth to combat inflation," he explained.

Layering Income Sources

Margaret, the Long-Lived Optimist, learned the importance of layering her income sources to sustain her lifestyle through decades of retirement. Her strategy included:

- **Guaranteed Income**: Social Security and an annuity provided a solid foundation.
- **Flexible Income**: Investments in bonds and dividend-paying stocks allowed her to cover unexpected expenses.
- **Growth-Oriented Income**: A portion of her savings remained in equities, ensuring her portfolio could outpace inflation.

This layered approach allowed Margaret to stretch her resources far beyond her initial retirement plan, giving her financial independence well into her 90s.

Actionable Steps to Build Your Income Stream

1. **Identify Your Income Needs**: Calculate your essential and discretionary expenses.
2. **Secure Guaranteed Income**: Use Social Security, pensions, and annuities to cover the basics.
3. **Add Flexibility**: Include dividend stocks, bond funds, or other investments that can provide variable income.
4. **Plan for Growth**: Keep a portion of your portfolio in growth-oriented investments to combat inflation.
5. **Regularly Review and Adjust**: Life and markets change; your income strategy should too.

By following these steps, you can create an income plan that supports your retirement goals, provides stability, and adapts to unforeseen challenges. Your retirement paycheck isn't just about money—it's about ensuring your financial security and freedom to enjoy this new chapter of life.

Working With Financial Professionals

Navigating retirement income strategies can be overwhelming, especially when trying to balance growth, income, and tax efficiency. This is where financial professionals come into play, but not all advisors are created equal. Understanding the difference between a traditional financial advisor and a retirement specialist is critical to ensuring your retirement plan meets your unique needs.

Growth Versus Income Focus

Traditional financial advisors, such as CFAs, often emphasize growth and accumulation strategies. Their expertise lies in building portfolios that maximize returns over the long term. While this approach works well during your working years, it can fall short in retirement when the focus shifts to income and decumulation. For example, Barbara, the Recent Retiree Adjuster, initially worked with a growth-focused advisor who didn't account for her need for steady income. After facing challenges with market volatility, she transitioned to a retirement specialist who tailored her portfolio to include guaranteed income sources like annuities.

Retirement specialists, on the other hand, focus on creating income streams that can withstand the unique risks of retirement, such as longevity, market volatility, and inflation. They consider strategies that ensure you don't outlive your money while balancing the need for flexibility. Michael, the Long-Term Visionary, valued this approach as he worked with a specialist to convert a portion of his traditional IRA to a Roth IRA, reducing future tax burdens and enhancing income predictability.

Tailored Strategies for Peace of Mind

For Susan, the Risk-Averse Safety Seeker, working with a retirement specialist provided the guidance she needed to ensure her essential expenses were covered by guaranteed income. Her advisor prioritized tools like fixed indexed annuities and inflation-protected securities, giving her the confidence to navigate retirement without worrying about market swings.

In contrast, Tom, the Near-Retiree Planner, initially hesitated to switch from his growth-focused advisor. However, as he approached retirement, he recognized the importance of transitioning to a decumulation strategy. A retirement specialist helped him layer his income sources, combining Social Security, annuities, and dividend-paying stocks to create a stable and flexible retirement paycheck.

Key Differences Between Advisors

Here's how a retirement specialist differs from a growth-focused financial advisor:

- **Focus**: Growth advisors prioritize capital appreciation; retirement specialists emphasize income stability and longevity.
- **Tools**: Growth advisors rely on equities and mutual funds; specialists incorporate annuities, Social Security optimization, and tax-efficient strategies.
- **Risk Management**: Specialists address risks like sequence of returns, longevity, and healthcare costs, which growth advisors may overlook.

Making the Right Choice

David and Lisa, the Established Retiree Optimizers, worked with both types of advisors. They found their CFA invaluable during their accumulation phase but relied on a retirement specialist to refine their income strategy. "It's about finding the right expert for each stage of life," Lisa explained.

When choosing a financial professional, ask specific questions about their experience with retirement income planning. Look for advisors who can integrate tax strategies, Social Security optimization, and guaranteed income tools into your plan. The right professional will not only secure your finances but also provide peace of mind as you navigate this new chapter.

Top 3 Items Readers Will Learn:

1. How to create a personalized implementation timeline based on your retirement situation and goals
2. Methods for selecting and working effectively with financial professionals
3. Strategies for monitoring and adjusting your plan as circumstances change

Having the knowledge to plan for retirement isn't enough - success comes from knowing how to put that knowledge into action through a comprehensive, personalized implementation strategy. This chapter provides the roadmap for turning retirement planning concepts into reality, ensuring you have both the blueprint and the tools needed to create and maintain a successful retirement plan.

Your Implementation Blueprint

Creating a successful retirement plan requires more than a collection of financial products—it demands a thoughtful, integrated strategy tailored to your unique goals and circumstances. From identifying what matters most to building a sustainable income stream and working with the right financial professionals, each step in this process lays the foundation for a secure and fulfilling retirement.

The experiences of Tom, Barbara, Susan, David and Lisa, Michael, and Margaret highlight the importance of aligning your plan with your priorities and adapting as your needs evolve. By focusing on decumulation strategies, optimizing guaranteed income, and addressing risks like inflation and taxes, you can confidently transition from saving for retirement to enjoying it.

Now that you've constructed your blueprint, the next step is to ensure it remains strong over time. A well-designed retirement plan is not static; it must evolve with changes in your life, the market, and tax laws. Monitoring and refining your strategy will be key to maintaining financial stability and peace of mind throughout your retirement years.

Conclusion: Your Path to Retirement Confidence

As you reach the conclusion of this book, one key message stands out: you have the power to create a secure, fulfilling, and adaptable retirement. The journey to financial independence and peace of mind may seem complex, but with the right strategies and guidance, it becomes manageable and rewarding. Retirement is not the end of a career—it's the beginning of a new phase of life, one filled with opportunities to live on your terms.

Throughout these pages, we've explored the essential elements of a modern retirement plan, from managing market volatility and ensuring guaranteed income to optimizing taxes and planning for longevity. By addressing these challenges head-on, you've gained the knowledge and tools needed to turn uncertainty into confidence.

The stories of Tom, Barbara, David and Lisa, Susan, Michael, and Margaret illustrate that while everyone's journey is unique, the principles of sound retirement planning remain universal. Tom showed us the importance of preparation, Barbara demonstrated the value of flexibility, and David and Lisa highlighted the need for tax efficiency and legacy planning. Susan's focus on security and Michael's long-term vision provided valuable insights, while Margaret's resilience reminded us to always plan for the unexpected.

Now, the next step is action. Knowledge alone doesn't secure a successful retirement—it's the application of what you've learned that makes all the difference. Begin by reviewing your current financial situation, identifying gaps in your plan, and prioritizing your goals. Build an income strategy that supports your essential expenses and safeguards your future, while remaining adaptable to life's changes.

Finally, remember that retirement is not just about financial security—it's about creating the freedom to enjoy life on your terms. Whether your dreams include travel, family time, or pursuing passions, the strategies in this book are designed to help you achieve them with confidence.

Retirement is your time to design, explore, and live fully. Take the lessons and tools from this book, commit to proactive planning, and embrace this new chapter with excitement and certainty. The future is yours to shape—start today.

Glossary of Terms

1. **401(k):** A retirement savings plan offered by employers that allows employees to contribute pre-tax income, with potential employer matching contributions.
2. **403(b):** A retirement plan similar to a 401(k), designed for employees of public schools, tax-exempt organizations, and certain ministers.
3. **Annuity:** A financial product that provides a series of payments at regular intervals, often used for retirement income.
4. **Adjusted Gross Income (AGI):** An individual's total gross income minus specific deductions, used to calculate taxable income.
5. **Asset Allocation:** The process of dividing investments among different asset categories like stocks, bonds, and cash to balance risk and reward.
6. **Beneficiary:** A person designated to receive benefits from a retirement account, insurance policy, or estate.
7. **Cash Reserve:** A liquid fund set aside for emergencies or short-term needs.
8. **Defined Benefit Plan:** A pension plan where the employer guarantees a specified monthly benefit upon retirement, based on factors like salary and years of service.
9. **Defined Contribution Plan:** A retirement plan where employees and/or employers contribute to an individual account, such as a 401(k).
10. **Dividend:** A portion of a company's earnings distributed to shareholders.
11. **Estate Planning:** Preparing tasks to manage an individual's asset base in the event of their incapacitation or death.

12. **Full Retirement Age (FRA):** The age at which a person can claim full Social Security benefits, determined by their birth year.
13. **Guaranteed Income:** Reliable, consistent payments, often from Social Security, pensions, or annuities, that provide financial stability.
14. **Health Savings Account (HSA):** A tax-advantaged medical savings account available to individuals enrolled in high-deductible health plans.
15. **Inflation:** The rate at which the general level of prices for goods and services rises, eroding purchasing power over time.
16. **Inflation-Protected Securities:** Investments, such as Treasury Inflation-Protected Securities (TIPS), designed to protect against inflation.
17. **IRA (Individual Retirement Account):** A tax-advantaged account for retirement savings, with options like Traditional IRA and Roth IRA.
18. **Longevity Risk:** The risk of outliving one's retirement savings due to increased life expectancy.
19. **Market Volatility:** Fluctuations in the market price of investments due to various economic factors.
20. **Medicare:** A federal health insurance program for people aged 65 and older or those with certain disabilities.
21. **Medigap:** Supplemental insurance that covers costs not included in original Medicare.
22. **Required Minimum Distributions (RMDs):** The minimum amount that must be withdrawn annually from tax-deferred retirement accounts starting at a specific age.
23. **Roth Conversion:** Moving money from a Traditional IRA or 401(k) into a Roth IRA to benefit from tax-free growth.

24. **Sequence of Returns Risk:** The risk of experiencing poor investment returns at the beginning of retirement when withdrawals are made.

25. **Social Security:** A federal program providing retirement, disability, and survivor benefits to eligible individuals.

26. **Tax Bracket:** A range of income subject to a specific tax rate.

27. **Tax Diversification:** Allocating savings among taxable, tax-deferred, and tax-free accounts to optimize tax efficiency.

28. **Tax-Efficient Withdrawal Strategy:** A plan to withdraw funds from various accounts to minimize taxes in retirement.

29. **Treasury Inflation-Protected Securities (TIPS):** Government bonds that adjust for inflation to protect purchasing power.

30. **Traditional IRA:** A retirement savings account with tax-deferred growth until withdrawals begin.

31. **Withdrawal Rate:** The percentage of retirement savings withdrawn annually, typically used to determine sustainable income.

32. **Long-Term Care Insurance:** Insurance designed to cover the costs of care needed due to chronic illness, disability, or aging.

33. **Hybrid Annuity:** A financial product combining annuity benefits with additional features, such as long-term care coverage.

34. **Income Rider:** An addition to an annuity that provides guaranteed income for life.

35. **Provisional Income:** Income used to determine if Social Security benefits are taxable.

36. **Income Floor:** The minimum guaranteed income required to cover essential expenses.

37. **Donut Hole:** A gap in Medicare Part D prescription drug coverage that requires beneficiaries to pay a larger share of drug costs.
38. **Personal Pension:** A retirement income stream created using annuities to mimic traditional pensions.
39. **Legacy Planning:** The process of managing and transferring wealth to heirs or charitable causes after death.
40. **Taxable Account:** An investment account where income and gains are subject to taxes annually.
41. **Indexing:** Linking investment returns or interest credits to a financial index like the S&P 500.
42. **Deferred Annuity:** An annuity where payments begin at a future date.
43. **Immediate Annuity:** An annuity where payments begin immediately after purchase.
44. **Fixed Indexed Annuity (FIA):** A type of annuity that provides returns based on a market index, with principal protection.
45. **Inflation Rider:** An add-on to a financial product that adjusts income payments for inflation.
46. **Income Gap:** The difference between guaranteed income and essential expenses.
47. **Combined Income:** The sum of adjusted gross income, non-taxable interest, and half of Social Security benefits, used to calculate taxes on Social Security.
48. **Open Enrollment:** A period during which individuals can make changes to their Medicare or insurance plans.
49. **Survivor Benefits:** Social Security payments made to the spouse or dependents of a deceased individual.
50. **Spousal Benefits:** Social Security payments available to the spouse of a retired or disabled worker.

For Additional Support:
We are here to help. Request your free Social Security Analysis and retirement Income Plan. If you would like personalized guidance in maximizing your Social Security benefits and creating a comprehensive retirement income strategy, please contact:

Boom Retirement Solutions

(888) 839-1611

SCAN TO SCHEDULE

AN APPOINTMENT

For a free copy of our other book "Maximizing Social Security Benefits" send an email to **jeff@boomretirement.com** and in the Subject Line write "Free Book Social Security."

Made in the USA
Monee, IL
28 May 2026

51181362R00075